PIT BULLS
& PIT BULL TYPE DOGS

82 DOGS THE MEDIA DOESN'T WANT YOU TO MEET

Melissa McDaniel

the photo book projects: book 3

the
photo book
projects

PRESENT DOG
P R E S S

PIT BULLS & PIT BULL TYPE DOGS | the photo book projects | Melissa McDaniel

Published in 2011 by Present Dog Press

Photographs & text copyright © 2011 Melissa McDaniel
Design & layout copyright © 2011 Present Dog Press
www.melissa-mcdaniel.com

the
photo book
projects

ISBN-13: 978-0-9845903-2-2
ISBN-10: 0-9845903-2-3

Designer: Melissa McDaniel

Printer: CPC Solutions

The text of this book was composed in Century Gothic.

Printed and Bound in the USA
10 9 8 7 6 5 4 3 2 1

PRESENT DOG
P   R   E   S   S

Present Dog Press, P.O. Box 454, New Hope, PA 18938 | presentdogpress.com

For my grandmother Elsymae Shepperd & my grandfather Tom Shepperd,

for Sadie,

for Egil Nilsson,

and for all pit bulls & pit bull type dogs worldwide
who have been abused, banned, fought, neglected, abandoned, euthanized,
overbred, or given up on, or who languish in shelters due to public ignorance & fear

INTRODUCTION
NO GROUP OF DOGS NEEDS OUR HELP MORE

When I first conceived of the idea of doing a series of dog photo books to educate people about issues affecting dogs, especially dogs that are misunderstood or mistreated, there was no doubt in my mind that I would dedicate an entire book to pit bulls. You only have to visit any local shelter to understand why. I don't know where you live—in a big town, a small town, out West, in the Midwest or down South—it doesn't matter. Chances are, if you live in the United States (U.S.) and head down to your local animal control, you will see dog after dog there that could be labeled a "pit bull." If you live in a city like Philadelphia, where I live, you will find shelters full of them.

Inbreeding, overbreeding, dog fighting and breed-specific legislation are just some of the issues affecting these dogs. However, their worst enemy, the one causing them the most harm, is public perception. Viewed as vicious, mean fighters with locking jaws and a thirst for blood, the public thinks these dogs are not to be trusted. People believe these dogs are your friends one minute, but that they can snap and turn aggressive toward humans in an instant, as if switches have been flipped in their heads. People believe they are ticking time bombs. It is these misconceptions that are causing pit bulls to languish in shelters all across the U.S.

When I hear myths like those, I cannot help but think how sharply those words contrast with the words I would use to describe the hundreds of pit bulls I have photographed over the years...all sweet, loyal, loving and absolutely adorable dogs. If I were going to stereotype pit bulls, I would say they are the group of dogs most likely to lick my face while I am photographing them. It is difficult for people who have spent any amount of time with these animals to understand why they have such a bad reputation. To me, and the people who share their lives with these dogs, pit bulls are dogs, just like any other.

WHAT EXACTLY IS A PIT BULL?
Pit bulls are not a breed or even a breed mix. Many rescues and advocacy groups define a "pit bull" as any one of the following breeds: American Pit Bull Terrier (APBT); American Staffordshire Terrier (AST); and Staffordshire Bull Terrier (SBT). Some groups include American Bullies, while others do not. Of those, only the ASTs and the SBTs are breeds recognized by the American Kennel Club (AKC).

Other groups, including the general public and the media, tend to use the term loosely. For them, the term "pit bull" is applied to an ever-expanding group of dogs that includes the breeds just mentioned, any of those breeds mixed with another dog and/or any dog with a certain look to him. This look varies depending on who you ask. All of the dogs in this book could be called pit bulls or pit bull type dogs, yet their appearances vary tremendously. As one shelter employee in Ohio said to me regarding which dogs could or could not be adopted out from his shelter: "If it looks like a pit bull, it's a pit bull."

OTHER BREEDS HAVE GOTTEN A BAD RAP IN THE PAST
Pit bulls are not the only dogs in history to get a bad rap. In the U.S., there is a cycle that starts with fear, hype, popularity, and then lack of training, socialization and basic care for these animals. This leads to certain breeds being labeled as the "vicious dog du jour." Once the dogs are labeled as "vicious," they become the "macho guy's dog to have," and so they are then in demand and the population increases even more. The hype attracts the wrong sort of owners: those who are not raising the dogs as family pets and who have little interest in socializing, training or providing adequate care for their dogs. Such is the case with pit bull type dogs at the moment.

Dog breeds in recent history that have experienced similar stereotyping:
- **19th century—Bloodhounds:** In the 1800s, Bloodhounds had a reputation as being a fearsome, bloodthirsty breed; however, the term "bloodhound" was loosely applied and encompassed over 10 distinctly separate Bloodhound breeds, in addition

to all mixes of those breeds. A number of disparate dogs were lumped into this group and labeled as "bloodhounds."

- **1910s-1940s—German Shepherds:** In 1925, German Shepherds were considered such a problem that the borough of Queens in New York City proposed a ban on them. Australia banned them in 1929.
- **1950s-1970s—Doberman Pinschers:** Dobermans earned their reputation as a dangerous breed after they became associated with the Nazis during World War II.
- **1980s-present—Pit Bulls:** By 2000, pit bull hysteria led to more than 200 U.S. towns banning them.

FAMILY PETS SUDDENLY DECLARED "VICIOUS & DANGEROUS"?

Pit bulls did not just appear in the U.S. during the last 30 years. They have been here, living alongside us as working dogs and family pets. Studio portraits of Victorian children standing next to pit bull type dogs are common. In fact, pit bulls in England were known as "nanny dogs" because they are so good with children. Pit bulls appear in advertisements and on television shows. Buster Brown's dog was a pit bull, and so was the dog Petey on the *Our Gang* (*The Little Rascals*) television show. Helen Keller's service dog was a pit bull, and Theodore Roosevelt had pit bulls as pets. Pit bull Stubby, a service dog during World War I, saved the lives of troops by alerting men to the smell of gas in the trenches and by barking to let paramedics know where wounded men were lying on the battlefields. Today, many celebrities, including Rachael Ray and Jessica Biel, share their lives with pit bulls.

So if pit bulls did not just suddenly appear in our communities, then why is it that we lived so peacefully with them before, but now they are feared and labeled as "vicious, dangerous" dogs? In Jim Gorant's *The Lost Dogs*, he writes: "In the mid-1970s, enterprising reporters began writing about the underground world of dog fighting.... This had the effect of promoting pit bulls as next in the line of tough-guy dogs....Between 1983 and 1984 the United Kennel Club (UKC) reported a 30 percent increase in registrations....Between 1966 and 1975 there was one newspaper account of a fatality that resulted from a pit bull attack. In 1986, pit bulls appeared in 350 newspaper, magazine and journal articles. Some of those reported legitimate pit bull attacks—the price of so many unsocialized, abused and aggressively trained dogs popping up around the country—but many were the result of pit bull hysteria, in which almost any incident involving a dog was falsely reported as a pit bull attack. The breed, which had existed in some form for hundreds of years, didn't suddenly lose control. The dogs simply fell into the hands of many more people who had no interest in control. By 2000, pit bull fear and hype had reached such proportions that the breed was banned in more than 200 cities and counties around the U.S. Lost in all the legislation was the fact that for decades the pit bull had been considered one of the most loyal, loving and people-friendly dogs on the planet."

The hype surrounding pit bull type dogs has led to myths and misinformation about APBTs, ASTs and SBTs. I address other myths later on in this book (*see pg. 154*); however, the main myth that these dogs are inherently vicious is unfounded. The APBT, AST and SBT pass the American Temperament Testing Society's (ATTS) temperament test at rates of 84.3 percent, 83.4 percent and 88.8 percent, respectively. Compare this to Golden Retrievers (84.2 percent), Great Danes (79.2 percent) and Weimaraners (80.1 percent). Carl Herkstroeter, the president of the ATTS, has commented on these results: "We have tested somewhere around 1,000 pit bull type dogs....I've tested half of them. And of the number I've tested I have disqualified one pit bull because of aggressive tendencies. They have done extremely well. They have a good temperament. They are very good with children."

As was the case with the word "bloodhound" in the 19th century, the term "pit bull" is being applied to a large group of dogs with disparate genetic compositions. **On the one hand, the dogs are being lumped into a group based on their appearance, and on the other hand, they are stereotyped and maligned as though they were a specific breed with certain genetic predispositions and traits.** Rather than stereotyping dogs, we should be treating them as individuals. However, to most people, and much of the media, a pit bull is any big, scary dog that bites. This incorrect labeling, the result of pit bull hysteria, has led to many incidents being falsely reported as pit bull attacks.

THE TRAGIC RESULT OF STEREOTYPING & THE SPREAD OF MISINFORMATION

The result of the media stereotyping, the hype and fear that surrounds pit bull type dogs and the discrimination against these dogs is tragic—a death sentence for many of these dogs who languish in shelters because people are afraid to adopt them, or who find themselves victims of local laws that ban them. Bans, higher euthanasia rates, fewer adoptions, animal cruelty, dog fighting, overbreeding and inbreeding are just a few of the issues.

Breed-specific legislation or laws (BSL). BSL, also called breed-discriminatory laws, is the term for laws that either regulate or ban certain breeds completely in the hope of reducing dog attacks. BSL ranges from mandatory muzzling of pit bull type dogs in some parts of the country, to forced removal and/or euthanasia in others. When bans are enacted, owners are forced to give up family pets or move.

The local governments conducting the bans disagree on what a pit bull type dog is, with a Miami-Dade county judge admitting that their local law was "too vague" and unenforceable. For example, do you ban a dog that is 50 percent pit bull? 20 percent? How do you know for sure what the dog's genetic makeup is? How do you determine which family pet can stay and which must leave the area or be euthanized? Looks? If this is the basis, then it is not actually "breed"-specific legislation, but "looks"-specific legislation. BSL varies across the U.S. In some areas the list of banned dogs includes many other breeds and mixes, such as American Bulldogs, Chow Chows, Dalmatians, Doberman Pinschers, German Shepherds, Mastiffs, any mix of these breeds or any dogs who simply resemble these breeds.

BSL has never resulted in a reduction in dog-related injuries, either in the U.S. or abroad. BSL sets neighbor against neighbor, discriminates against responsible owners, creates unsolvable enforcement problems for animal control officers, wastes precious public resources and fails to address problematic owner behavior. All dog owners have an unequivocal responsibility for the humane care (including proper diet, veterinary care, socialization and training), custody (including licensing and microchipping) and control of their dogs. The alternative solution for many states, including New York, Texas and Illinois, has been to favor laws that identify, track and regulate dangerous dogs individually, regardless of breed, and prohibit BSL.

Fewer adoptions & higher euthanasia rates. Pit bulls have a greater chance of being euthanized than other types of dogs. The fear and hype has created an unwillingness by the public to adopt these dogs. As a result, thousands of pit bull type dogs languish in shelters across the U.S. Sweet, obedient, friendly, fun dogs are overlooked due to public ignorance and fear. Many live for months in a stressful shelter environment, if they make it out at all. Six to 8 million cats and dogs enter U.S. shelters each year, and half are euthanized, with a large percentage of them being pit bull type dogs.

Misguided shelter policies, insurance company policies & BSL are to blame for some shelters & rescues refusing to admit or adopt out pit bull type dogs. The reasons for these situations vary; however, some shelters do not adopt them out because of BSL, while others refuse to accept them. Many rescues restrict the number they take in, knowing the expense they will incur to keep these dogs for months on end and also knowing that they can rescue and rehome several non-pit bull dogs in the same time frame it typically takes to adopt out one pit bull type dog. In addition, some rescues do not accept pit bull type dogs because their insurance will not cover these dogs.

Dog fighting—victims of cruelty. Because these dogs are labeled as "vicious" and seen as "the tough guy's dog," people who do not view dogs as family are attracted to them. They leave these dogs unsocialized, chained outdoors and with inadequate care. These dogs are often victims of cruelty and/or victims of dog fighting. In dog fighting, female dogs are bred too often and with little regard for their health. Rape stands are used to hold non-receptive females in place for mating. Some dogs are used as bait dogs to test the fighting ability of other dogs. In the past, dogs from fight busts were seized, often remaining in isolation for months or even years, held as evidence until their perpetrators' trials were over. They had little interaction with the outside world. This isolation took a psychological toll on the dogs, especially those who were very young, since this lack of exposure during their critical stages of development, left them scared of all they had yet to experience (*see Uba, pgs. 138 & 139; & Alan, pg. 46*). It was common practice, after the trials were over, for all of the dogs to be euthanized. Since 2008, dog fighting has been a felony offense in all 50 U.S. states.

Overbreeding & inbreeding. The high demand for these dogs is causing people to breed these dogs for profit, with little concern for the dogs' health and/or the quality of dog being produced. These backyard breeders are often creating dogs with many health issues. Cuda (*see pgs. 54 & 55*) has deformities believed to have been caused by inbreeding. She was purchased from a backyard breeder in North Carolina before she found her forever home. Through DNA testing, she was shown to be 100 percent SBT.

THE DOGS IN THIS BOOK
I wanted the dogs in this book to represent the group of dogs in the U.S. that is commonly referred to now as "pit bull type dogs." This book does not focus on ASTs, APBTs and SBTs. Rather, the dogs in this book represent the ever-expanding group of dogs known as pit bull type dogs. This book uses the term "pit bull" to refer to this group of dogs. These dogs are one of the aforementioned breeds or some combination of them, a mix of those dogs with another dog breed or breeds, or simply dogs that have a certain look. That look varies depending on who is making the judgment. The dogs in this book have all been called pit bulls or pit bull mixes; however, their appearances vary tremendously. In addition, I have also included other breeds often mistakenly called "pit bulls," such as American Bulldogs and American Bulldog mixes. What these dogs actually are—that is, what their DNA actually is—for the purposes of this book is irrelevant. My idea was to compile a group of dogs that represent the group labeled as "pit bulls" (pit bull type dogs). My concern is that these dogs, if they found themselves in a shelter tomorrow, would be viewed as pit bulls and as a result would have a difficult time getting adopted, if they made it out at all. These are the dogs that are discriminated against. These are the dogs that need our help.

All of the dogs in this book are rescues—adopted from shelters or rescues, found as strays or rehomed—so, with a few exceptions, owners can only guess as to the genetic makeup of these dogs. Most DNA tests for dogs have shown us that a dog's genetic composition often differs drastically from what the dog's physical appearance would have you believe the dog is. I once knew a dog that was half APBT and half Chihuahua. The dog's owner knew for certain because her brother's APBT gave birth to the dog. The dog looked like a slightly larger version of a Chihuahua. I would never have guessed the dog had any other breed in him except Chihuahua. After I met that dog, I stopped stating with any confidence what I thought the genetic makeup was of any rescued dog. For these reasons, I have omitted all breed references for the dogs in this book. What is important, for the purposes of this book, is how these dogs look: they are labeled as "pit bull type dogs" ***because*** of the way they look.

Shelters, towns, politicians, governments, insurance companies, doggy day cares and others discriminate against this group of dogs because these dogs have a "pit bull look" about them. However, the dogs they are discriminating against may have a much smaller amount of APBT, AST or SBT in their genetic makeup than their looks would suggest, while other dogs that have a non-"pit bull type dog" look may have a much higher genetic composition of APBT, AST or SBT than their looks would suggest. Dogs like Centje (*see pgs. 114 & 115*), who has a "pit bull shaped head," may very well be 50 percent or more pit bull. However, since Centje has the Pointer- or Dalmatian-like body, he is unlikely to be discriminated against as a pit bull. Other dogs, ones with a bully look, who may have no DNA from ASTs, APBTs or SBTs, may in fact be labeled as "pit bulls." Oogy (*see pgs. 16 & 17*), for example, believed now to be a Dogo Argentino, was originally labeled a "pit bull" by the rescuers and the veterinary hospital that saved him. Choppers (*see pgs. 92 & 93*) was called a "pit bull" by a neighbor, but Choppers most likely has none of those breeds in him; he only has a certain look.

THIS PROJECT
Many people have asked me what it has been like traveling the country to photograph pit bulls. I was eager to get started, since I think many pit bull type dogs are some of the most fun to photograph. Most have incredibly

expressive faces and are athletic, playful and eager to please. The shoots were held in venues and a few in people's homes. I tried to combine as many shoots in one location as possible. This time around things went more smoothly. On the previous trips for the last two books, I stopped at many shelters and rescues around the country. As rewarding as it is to meet so many people doing what they can to help homeless animals, it can also, as one would expect, be depressing. For me to see kennels full of unwanted dogs in town after town was heartbreaking, especially since I knew that some of those dogs were not going to make it out of there. On those trips, I saw firsthand how many pit bull type dogs fill U.S. shelters and just how much they need our help. As upsetting as those trips were, I am grateful for them since they were the impetus for this project.

On the road trips I took to photograph for this book, I met some amazing people, who have dedicated their lives to these dogs, who have transformed dogs from frightened and traumatized to confident and social, and who take the time not only to make sure their dogs are all they can be, but also to make sure the world knows about it. I met people who are proud and happy to share their lives with these dogs. I met people who are devoted to pit bull type dogs, who speak out for the "breed," who foster dogs in their homes, who rescue pit bull type dogs and who love these dogs deeply. In fact, after meeting so many people who were fanatical about pit bulls, it was easy to forget that anyone dislikes them!

Many people I met on the trip told me they have noticed far more supporters of pit bulls than haters. I loved this quote from Martha Kennedy, whose dogs Vixen & Ziggy (see pgs. 86-89) are in this book, about what it is like to walk around town with your pit bulls:

"There are pit bull lovers everywhere! I've had women in stiletto heels come hobbling across traffic to love on my pitties, I've had others pull out their cell phones to show me pictures of their pit bull—after an evening of going to art openings,...my sister asked, "Is it always like this?" after the eighth person ran up to us to say 'hello' to my pit bull!"

I met some fantastic pit bull type dogs, too, who are educating people daily just by being themselves. I have met champions of canine disc, therapy dogs, service dogs, deaf dogs, victims of cruelty, victims of dog fighting, dogs who have earned their Canine Good Citizen certificates, "ambassadogs," certified therapy dogs, those that perform in numerous canine sports, and I have also met complete couch potatoes. They were all fantastic dogs in their own right. Most were total hams, while others were a little more shy about getting their photos taken, but all were lovable, sweet dogs and great family pets. I firmly believe the best educators are the dogs themselves.

A definite highlight for me was the chance to meet so many of the Vick dogs (see pgs. 132-153). These dogs were seized from NFL quarterback Michael Vick's property in 2007. I talk more at length later on in the book (see pgs. 132 & 133) about how these dogs and this case have altered the country's opinion of pit bulls and of dogs seized from fight busts. They have changed how fight bust dogs are treated, and because of them, most of these dogs are now given a chance at life. The Vick dogs are remarkable, beautiful examples of what it means to forgive, to trust, to persevere, to be resilient, to adapt and to enjoy and love life.

The most rewarding aspect of this project has been to hear people say how their dogs, the dogs I photographed, changed their minds about pit bulls. A number of people said they were initially hesitant about adopting a pit bull, but for some reason, they took that chance and have been rewarded for it ever since. They then became aware of the plight of pit bulls. Often, those same people are the staunchest advocates, taking every chance to meet and talk to people when they are out, or even attending rescue or advocacy events so they can educate people. Some volunteer at rescues, foster pit bulls in their homes and often involve their dogs in as many activities as possible—from canine sports to therapy work—just so they can show the world what pit bulls can do.

It is good for all of us to confront and overcome obstacles, stereotypes and fears in our own lives; we grow in the process. Of the people who adopted the dogs in this book, many did so even though they were not quite sure about pit bulls (or elderbulls, or victims of cruelty and dog fighting, etc.). Still, they took that chance, and their horizons, and the horizons of the people around them, were broadened because of it; it is a beautiful ripple effect. This applies to other rescued dogs, as well. It is easy to look at a fluffy, 8-week-old Golden Retriever puppy and think, "I want this dog." It is far less easy though to look at a mangy, emaciated or heartworm-positive dog, or unwanted dog, pit bull type dog (if you are afraid of them), or a scar-covered dog seized from a dog fighting bust and think, "This is the dog for me!" Still, many of the people in this book did that and never looked back. A great example is Kim Wolf, who saw the potential in a 14-year-old pit bull type dog seized from a cruelty case, a dog many people had overlooked, a dog many thought would never be adopted. That dog was Sarge (*see pgs. 130 & 131*), who went on to become a wonderful family pet, therapy dog and humane educator and who inspired people to rescue dogs, adopt pit bull type dogs, have compassion for animals and older pit bulls or "elderbulls" (and older dogs in general), and to join "Team Sarge" to show support for these causes. Kim said, "Sarge taught us that while a shelter dog's kennel card or Petfinder description might place heavy significance on where a dog has been, most dogs are only focused on where they're going. It's up to us to bring them there." We give them a home and love, and they give us so much more in return, including educating us that they are more than their past, than their breed, than their age, than their disability....

Is the world getting better for pit bulls? Many people in this book said if they are out walking their dogs, others coming toward them will cross the street to avoid them. They have had trouble finding doggy day cares that accept pit bull type dogs, and their dogs were not accepted at certain locations as humane educators, reading-assistance dogs or therapy dogs because of their "breed." Shelters in certain cities, such as Denver and Houston, do not adopt out pit bull type dogs. All of that said, though, if you are a part of the pit bull rescue and advocacy world, I think it must feel like things are getting better. The number of supporters out there is growing. Lily (*see pg. 50*) was recently the first pit bull type dog allowed into her shelter's foster program. The Cleveland Animal Protective League, the largest humane organization in the state of Ohio, just adopted out a pit bull type dog, which ended the decades-long ban on pit bull adoptions from this shelter. In June 2011, the Cleveland City Council voted to amend part of the City's vicious dog ordinance, stating that the "pit bull breed" will no longer be considered "vicious." Thanks to the Vick dogs, dogs seized from dog fighting busts are now evaluated as individuals and given a chance at life rather than across-the-board euthanasia. Pit bull type dogs are even appearing in the national advertising campaigns of major brands. All of these changes give us hope for these dogs.

As much as this book is about happy endings, about dogs who may have had a rough start in life, but have wound up in their forever homes, this book is for those who never were so lucky—those who were euthanized, abused, abandoned, thrown away. I am creating this book for them, and in the hope that things will change for dogs in the future. The photos and stories in this book show the dogs I know—the dogs that are happy, playful, goofy, sweet, loving and loyal companions. I hope to change attitudes and spark a change for the better for these dogs. I want this book to show what I know—and what the people who share their lives with these dogs know—that pit bulls are dogs, just like any others.

And lastly, for the photo of the main section of the book (*see pg. 10*), I chose a photo of Hector. Hector is a happy dog with an unhappy past. He was one of the Michael Vick pit bulls (*see pgs. 140 & 141*). Needless to say, his time at Bad Newz Kennels was not a party. Hector wears terrible scars across his chest yet wears a big, goofy grin across his face. He has no issues, has earned his Canine Good Citizen certificate, has been temperament tested and is a certified therapy dog. He loves people, dogs and kids. His beauty lies in his refusal to focus on his past and his determination to enjoy all he has today. He loves playing, his treats, a good belly rub and his new family. He has an extraordinary spirit that he refused to let be broken. When I think of Gilda Radner's quote—"Dogs are the most amazing creatures; they give unconditional love. For me they are the role model for being alive."—I think of Hector. He is not only a reminder to us of how we should live our lives, but also a reminder of what it is about dogs that makes us love them so much. Hector gives us all hope not only for pit bull type dogs but also for rescued dogs in general. Hector, with his happy face and resilient spirit, is a great introduction to the dogs in this book.

For more information on pit bull type dogs, please refer to the Pit Bull Myths & Resources section (see pg. 154).
The facts in the introduction of this book were taken from The Lost Dogs by Jim Gorant & The Pit Bull Placebo by Karen Delise.

Dogs should be treated as individuals
and should not be stereotyped by their
breed, their "handicap" or their past.
Judge them for who they are, not for
what others have told you they are.

MELISSA MCDANIEL

PIT BULLS
& PIT BULL TYPE DOGS
82 DOGS THE MEDIA DOESN'T WANT YOU TO MEET

In the dogs' biographies: *If a dog lives with another dog that did not come from the same litter, the dog is referred to in quotes as the dog's "sister," "brother" or "sibling." If the dogs are actual littermates or blood relatives, then there are no quotation marks around mother, sister, brother, etc. Some of the participants asked that only their first names be used, and so their surnames have been omitted, others asked that their locations not be mentioned, and so the locations for those dogs have been omitted. I've left out labels for breeds for these dogs. They are all rescues and so it is anyone's guess as to what they truly are. What matters for the purposes of this book is that these dogs all have a certain look, and that they, and all other similar dogs around the world, are labeled as "pit bulls" because of the way they look and experience discrimination because of that label.*

JACK

GREAT WITH CATS, OTHER DOGS, PEOPLE & KIDS, JACK IS A VERY CUDDLY & AFFECTIONATE DOG
ADOPTED FROM PENNSYLVANIA SPCA (PSPCA)

Philadelphia Phillies second baseman Chase Utley & his wife, Jennifer, adopted Jack from the PSPCA, where Jennifer is a board member. Jack's parents were both confiscated from a dog fighting bust in 2008. It was one of the bigger cruelty cases in PSPCA recent history. His mother gave birth to a litter of 11 puppies in the shelter and was extremely loving to all of them. Unfortunately, due to the horrific conditions and life she endured at the hands of humans, she was protective of herself and her puppies and seen as a risk to any future owner. She had to be humanely euthanized. The Utleys met Jack at a photo shoot they were doing for *Philadelphia* magazine and decided to adopt him. They described him as "a little blob" among his littermates. That little blob has become a very handsome dog—so handsome, in fact, that he has become quite a celebrity himself. Jack's credits include appearing in the movie *Cop Out*, modeling in a photo shoot for *Marie Claire*, appearing in the national "Adopt, Don't Buy" campaign for PETA, and being featured on the cover of the Phillies' "Save a Pet at the Park" calendar. When he is not busy being a star, he loves playing with his dog friends, Roxie & Potter, playing fetch, hiking, going to the ballpark with Chase and playing with all the guys, and eating baseballs. In 2011, the couple established the Utley Foundation to bring awareness to the growing epidemic of animal cruelty. Its mission is "to educate the community in the proper treatment of animals and raise funds for the fight against animal neglect, pain and suffering."

ZUFFA

CONNECTICUT
ZUFFA LOVES EVERYBODY—EVEN IF SOMEONE IS NOT INTERESTED IN HIM, HE KEEPS TRYING
AKA FAFA, FAFALAF, ZOOEY, ZOOFALOOF & FAFFER
ADOPTED FROM COMPANION PET RESCUE & TRANSPORT (CPR)

Zuffa's mom was found running free in Tennessee. CPR found her and took her in, where she gave birth to a litter of puppies. Emily & Christian Anton had just bought their first house, and after only two weeks of living in a dogless home, they decided to start looking for a dog online. They found Lucas, one of those puppies, online, but he was already spoken for, so the rescue sent them a photo of Lucas's brother Zuffa, who had not been posted online yet. He was just 10 weeks old. They fell in love with him, and had Zuffa transported to them in Connecticut. When they first got Zuffa, Emily's mother was not sure what to think. The first time he kissed her, she said, "I've never kissed a pit bull before!" That was the first of many kisses to come. Their families have fallen in love with their dogs, and their parents have become advocates for the "breed." Zuffa lives a charmed life: he has a basket full of toys and gets to sleep on the couch all day. He loves everyone and loves giving kisses. Zuffa enjoys playing with his "sister" (*see pgs. 30 & 31*) and his "grandmother's" two dogs, Cline & Mel. Zuffa, particular about his sleeping situation, will nest on the couch and scratch the blankets until they are just right, which usually takes him several tries. At bedtime, Zuffa will stare at Emily & Chris until they go upstairs with him. Zuffa's favorite treats are green beans. He always takes his green bean to the rug in the living room to savor it.

OOGY

PENNSYLVANIA
OOGY & LARRY VISIT SCHOOLS & ATTEND EVENTS TO RAISE AWARENESS & FUNDS FOR ANIMAL RESCUE
AKA OOGYBOY, PHATTY DOG, THE OOGSTER, MR. HAPPY DOG, RUHROH, WOOWOO & WOO DOGGY
ADOPTED FROM ARDMORE ANIMAL HOSPITAL (AAH)

Larry & Jennifer Levin and their sons, Noah & Dan, were not looking for a dog. They had gone to AAH to say goodbye to their cat and wound up saying hello to a rambunctious "pit bull." The dog barreled the boys over with kisses after breaking away from a staff member. It seems as though the dog picked them. They adopted him and named him "Oogy" because the name sounded like "ugly," which is how the dog seemed to them at the time. Oogy had been used as a bait dog. He had only one ear, was missing a part of his lower left jawbone, and had a mound of pink scar tissue on his head due to the trauma. During a drug bust, the police found Oogy lying in a cage, where he had been left to die. Dr. Bianco, who operated on Oogy after the police brought him in to AAH for medical attention, estimated Oogy lay there without food, water or medicine, fully infected and bleeding to death for up to a week. Larry has often wondered, "What kept this dog, who had never known human kindness, going?" And he says he now knows: "He was waiting for us." It is impossible to meet Oogy and not go away feeling better than you did before you met him. Here is a dog who has been through hell and back and was only ever abused by people before being rescued, yet the words "gentle," "kind" and "loving" are inadequate to describe how Oogy is with other dogs, people and children. He is forgiveness and goodness incarnate. Oogy has more than a few lessons to teach us. Larry admits that until the moment he met Oogy and was told he was a pit bull, you could not have gotten him into the same room with one. Now, he & Oogy visit schools, where Larry tells students what he has learned: "That disliking a dog solely because of its breed is no more justifiable than it is to dislike a person because of his or her ethnicity." He continues, "Through Oogy I have learned that there are a lot more people doing great things for dogs. They don't get the same press as those doing bad things,...but they are out there, working wonders one dog at a time." Larry's love for this dog inspired him to write Oogy's story, *Oogy: The Dog Only a Family Could Love*, which spent 10 weeks on the *New York Times* best-seller list and has been published in eight countries.

16

CRASH

COLORADO
A BIG-TIME SNORER, SQUIRREL CHASER & GREAT PIT BULL AMBASSADOR
ADOPTED FROM A RESCUE THAT IS NO LONGER IN EXISTENCE

Crash was found walking down the street in Rome, GA, with a piece of rope tied to his collar. Just as he was about to step into traffic, a girl yelled out to stop him. He turned away from the road and ran toward her. She named him Crash since he had almost gotten into one. Her mother did not want a pit bull, so the girl took him to a rescue, whose owner was not happy to see a pit bull either, since they are hard to adopt out, but she accepted him. Roberto Eaton went to the rescue looking for a friend for his dog, Bear. He was not looking for a pit bull, since he had heard so many bad things, but when he saw Crash, he knew he was the one. Crash & Bear have been inseparable since. Now in Colorado, the dogs have the perfect life with Roberto & his wife, Marta, going hiking often. Roberto has seen discrimination, however, including people who would not rent to someone with a pit bull, and a boarding facility that denied Crash because of his "breed." Roberto convinced the facility to test Crash's temperament, and he passed with flying colors. The facility has since changed its policy. "I have had many people pull their young children off of him...as soon as I utter the words 'pit bull.' Never mind that they had their arms wrapped around his neck, or that he was gently licking the chocolate milk...off their faces." Roberto always takes the chance to educate people, which is easy since cute and lovable Crash changes minds everywhere he goes.

19

DUNCAN

PENNSYLVANIA
A CROWD ALWAYS GATHERS TO SEE DUNCAN AT THE NURSING HOME WHERE CAROL'S MOTHER RESIDES
ADOPTED FROM STAFFORDSHIRE BULL TERRIER CLUB OF AMERICA (SBTCA) (SBT RESCUE)

Picked up several times in poor condition by animal control, Duncan was skinny, had sores, parasites, hair loss and an old scar from an embedded collar—all indicating that he probably lived outdoors. During his last time at animal control he went unclaimed, and so the facility contacted the rescue arm of SBTCA to take him. Carol & John soon adopted him, and now he lives the good life on 17 acres and spends two hours each day hiking. He had to get used to home life and learn to feel safe enough to roll over for belly rubs. Because of his history, John & Carol were afraid he was a runner, but he turned out to be an obedient homebody. With little training, he now does not cross a threshold without permission and sits and waits outside to be leashed before his daily walks. Duncan spends his days at the couple's art gallery, where he works as the official greeter. He waits for a cue from customers as to how dog friendly they are. Once he gets the go ahead, he licks them, rolls over, brings them toys and sits on their feet. When not at the gallery, this dog-about-town visits a few of the outdoor cafés that John & Carol frequent and is well-known at some of the trendier restaurants. John & Carol have spent hours dispelling the negative stereotypes. Duncan's gentle demeanor and behavior, in spite of his unhappy past, never fail to amaze and impress people who had negative opinions of these dogs. He is a great ambassador for bullies and rescued dogs in general.

20

AMBER

NEW JERSEY
CHANGING PEOPLE'S MINDS ABOUT PIT BULLS EVERY DAY SINCE 2002
AKA AMBERLINA, MOMMA & DADDY'S GIRL
ADOPTED FROM PITTY RESCUE (JEFF'S RESCUE)

Jeff Coltenback met a girl from a downtrodden neighborhood who was going to breed her new puppy once the dog was old enough. Jeff was not going to let that happen. He convinced the girl to give him the dog. That dog came to be known as Amber Honey Star. Jeff has been rescuing, rehabilitating and rehoming pit bulls since 2000. He saved Amber, just as he had saved many others before her. However, instead of rehoming Amber, he kept her. He could tell Amber was different. He knew she would make a great therapy dog and help change people's minds about pit bulls. Amber likes the usual games that dogs like, but what Amber loves most is going on therapy visits. She loves making people feel better. When Jeff asks her whether she wants to go to work, she gets excited. On one of their first therapy visits, Amber met a blind woman who was in a deep depression and had not smiled or interacted with anyone in three months. The woman also was not fond of dogs. Not only did Amber change the woman's mind about dogs, but she smiled and lit up with Amber by her side. In addition to the hundreds of therapy visits over the years, Jeff & Amber have made countless visits to Boy Scouts, Girl Scouts and summer camps, where they teach children how to properly interact with dogs. People love her. Jeff said, "This is one pit bull you'll never hear about on the news. And, that's unfortunate, because she is a great ambassador for her 'breed!' I love her dearly."

KEIKO

TEXAS
KEIKO IS HAPPY TO LET HER 9-LB., 14-YEAR-OLD "SISTER" BOSS HER AROUND
FOUND AS A STRAY

A friend of Denise Buckheister & Michael Smith had seen a large dog running along a busy highway and then later on saw the same dog outside her office building. Afraid the dog would wind up at the local shelter, which had a reputation for not being welcoming to bully breeds, she called Denise to rescue her. Denise came to get her, and lovable Keiko quickly became part of her family. "Keiko is one of the sweetest dogs we've ever been lucky enough to have in our lives. She's loving, sensitive and cuddly. She also does not understand why anyone would *not* want to pet her or love her." Keiko, who was about 3 years old when Denise & Michael adopted her, had an abdominal scar that Denise thought was a spay scar until Keiko went into heat. So it seems someone had cared enough about her in the past to have an operation performed on her. Keiko is now spayed and living the good life. She shares her house with five other dogs (see pgs. 26 & 27), who all play well together and are lost without one another. While Keiko loves to run around and wrestle with the other dogs, she also thoroughly enjoys lying on a recliner all day when possible. She is a 65-lb. lapdog, curling up into a very tiny ball on people's laps to sleep. She loves to snuggle, to snore, to chew on very large nylabones and to zoom around the house wanting you to chase her. A real lovebug, she just wants to cuddle. She likes everyone she meets, which is written all over her extremely expressive face.

TAFFY

TEXAS
TAFFY IS OBSESSED WITH TENNIS BALLS, PLAYING FETCH & SOCCER
ADOPTED FROM EULESS ANIMAL CONTROL (EAC) & HOMEWARD BOUND ANIMAL RESCUE (HBAR)

A friend of Denise Buckheister & Michael Smith found Taffy as a stray. He called animal control, which took possession of her and held her for the mandatory three-day hold before she could be adopted out. When Denise first saw her at the shelter, Taffy was very thin. After the three-day hold was over, Denise picked her up to be adopted out through HBAR, but Denise & Michael wound up falling in love with her and adopted her themselves. Taffy is very good around other dogs. She now has two large "sisters" (see pgs. 24 & 25) and two large "brothers" to play with, and one little 9-lb. "sister" who just bosses her around. Taffy loves to go for car rides, take walks, wrestle with her "brothers" and "sisters," and lie in Denise's lap. She enjoys going to the baseball stadium to see Michael at work and to visit his co-workers. Active and athletic, Taffy loves to play fetch and soccer. Taffy also smiles very often, a big, open-mouth smile. She is now a normal weight and is the stunningly beautiful dog she was meant to be, and is in the great, loving home she always deserved.

LUNA

NEW JERSEY
LUNA THINKS THAT EVERYONE IS A FRIEND & WILL SIT ON PEOPLE'S LAPS & LICK THEIR EARS
AKA LOONEY TUNES
ADOPTED FROM PET RESCUE OF MERCER (PRM)

Luna was found in a cooler with three littermates during a drug bust in Philadelphia. Even though she was around 4 weeks old, she and her littermates were already eating dry food. Luna was considered the runt of the litter. Friends of Emma & Marc Stewart adopted her brother Petey. They had invited Emma & Marc to meet Petey and showed them pictures of Luna at her foster home. Emma & Marc fell in love with Luna and soon adopted her. Luna has playdates with Petey once a month or more. She adapted very well to living in their house, with their five cats and teenage son. She loves to play with the cats; she will steal their toys to get them to chase her, and when they catch her she will snuggle with them and clean their heads and ears. Everyone in the family adores her. Luna often visits Marc's grandfather and lifts his spirits with a kiss and a snuggle. She has her own loveseat to chew her bones on. Entertaining and fun, Luna enjoys running in the yard, lying in the sun when it is not too hot, spinning in a circle while standing and sleeping on the bed like a human with her head on the pillow. She also adores all kids and dogs. A very loving and sensitive dog, she seems to know when a family member is not feeling well and will hang out with that person more on those days. Luna is one happy, friendly, snuggly, loving puppy.

PETEY

NEW JERSEY
AT A LOCAL FAIR, PETEY RECENTLY LAY ON HIS SIDE TO LET FIVE KIDS PET HIM
AKA MERLE, MERLIE, STASH, STASH-N-BASH, MERLIE STASH, PETEY STASH & MEGA STASH
ADOPTED FROM PET RESCUE OF MERCER (PRM)

At 4 weeks old, Petey and three of his siblings were rescued from a house during a drug raid in Philadelphia. After they were picked up by the police, they were brought to PRM. Two of the volunteers separated the puppies between them and brought them home to foster. Petey's foster mom put the dogs on Petfinder.com, which is how Frank & Nicole Gallo found them. After meeting both of the then 2-month-old puppies, they decided on Petey. They adopted him on the spot. When the puppies said goodbye, they gave each other very gentle kisses. So touched by that, Frank & Nicole spread the word about Petey's sister Luna to everyone they knew, and their good friends adopted her. Frank & Nicole did not discover Petey was deaf until he was almost 3 months old. They had trained him with verbal commands and hand signals, and it took Petey's obliviousness to the fire alarm going off in their home for them to realize that he could not hear. Petey is very social and loves all children, people and dogs. He does his part to educate others about pit bulls and deaf dogs by just being himself. He won over their neighbor, who, before meeting Petey, believed that all pit bulls, end up aggressive. He recently said he was wrong; every time he sees Petey he gets on his knees to get kisses. Petey lives a full life and is not bothered by his deafness. He knows over 30 commands.

DYNA

CONNECTICUT
SHE WAGS HER TAIL SO HARD WHEN SHE SEES PEOPLE/DOGS THAT SHE HITS HERSELF IN THE FACE
AKA NANA, NANNERS, DYNA-BO-BYNA, LITTLE GIRL, BABY GIRL, SWEETIE PIE, CUTIE PATOOTIE & BEANER
ADOPTED FROM SMILIN' PIT BULL RESCUE (SPBR)

Eric, the founder of SPBR, got an email saying that a box of pit bull mix puppies was dropped off by some young kids from a low-income household. The shelter could not take them in because of breed-specific legislation that banned them. So Eric took them in and brought them from Ohio to New York. Emily & Christian Anton decided to start looking for another dog when their dog Zuffa (*see pgs. 14 & 15*) was about to turn 1 year old. After some searching online, they came across SPBR, which had a bunch of puppies available, so they drove to New York to make a final decision. They swear that Dyna chose them. Her sister Bee was also a possibility, but Dyna just settled into Chris' arms. He looked at Emily and said, "This is the one." She was just 12 weeks old. Dyna is a very happy dog. When she first meets someone, she gives them a bunch of kisses and tail wags, and then she rolls over for belly rubs. Dyna loves everybody—dogs, adults and children. She seems to understand kids and is very gentle with them. Emily brought Dyna to the March for Babies, where Dyna walked alongside a stroller that had a 2-year-old girl in it. She kept checking in on the toddler and seemed to be making sure she was OK. Dyna loves to chase tennis balls, and one of Dyna's favorite things to do is chase bubbles. Calm Dyna tolerates Zuffa, even letting him clean her ears and nibble her ankles.

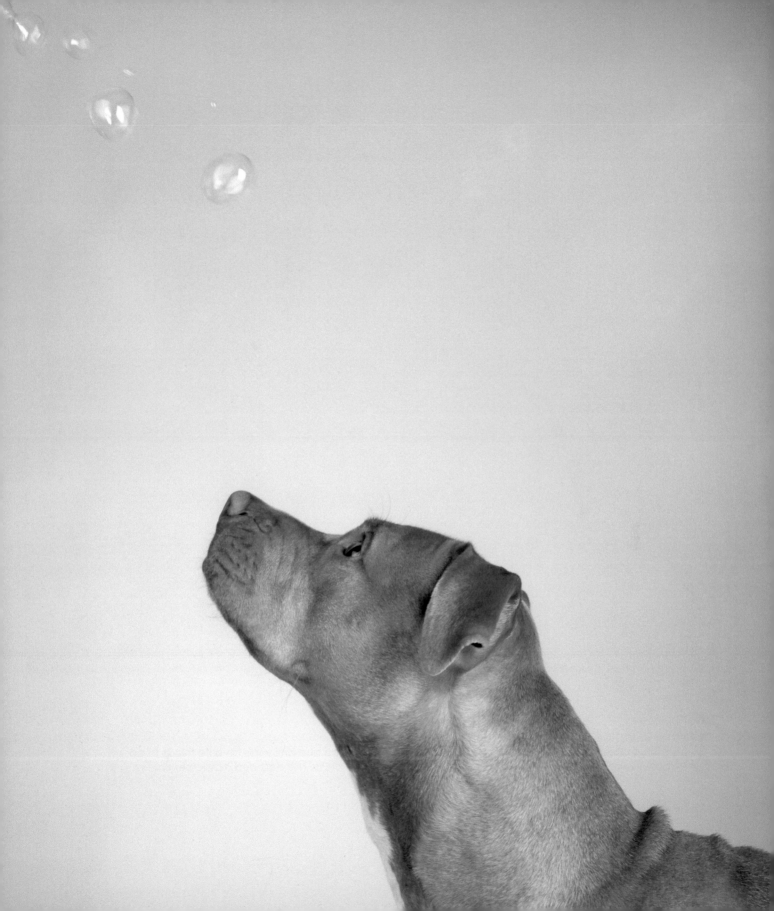

ISABELLA HOPE

CONNECTICUT

ISABELLA OFTEN VISITS DEBORAH, HER FOSTER MOM, WHO SHE IS ALWAYS ECSTATIC TO SEE
ADOPTED FROM OXFORD ANIMAL SHELTER (OAS)

Thrown away and left to die, Isabella was found lying in someone's yard. She had been abused and was emaciated. She could hardly breathe and could not stand up. She was given immediate medical attention, but it did not look like she was going to make it through the night. Isabella had been so overbred and neglected that her uterus was gangrenous. Miraculously, she survived, and when her health stabilized, she was fostered through OAS by Deborah Martin. Deborah loved and cared for Isabella and started her on her rehabilitation. Tara Patrick knew pit bulls were great dogs and was looking for an ambassador for the "breed" when she came across and adopted Isabella and continued her rehabilitation. Today, Isabella still faces challenges, including suffering from seizures. She is not a typical active pit bull: she is very calm and moves slowly. During the first two years of her life, she never had the chance to just "be a dog," but she is learning now. At first, she had a hard time warming up to people; if they patted her on her head, she cringed. She has come far. Isabella is one happy dog now. She is getting certified as a therapy dog, and she is so well behaved that she does not need to be walked on leash. Tara walks her with Isabella's BFF, her "sister" Lily Pad. People are often surprised to see a pit bull walking so calmly with a Maltese. Sweet and friendly with everyone she meets, especially children, Isabella lives happily with five dogs, two cats and a few birds.

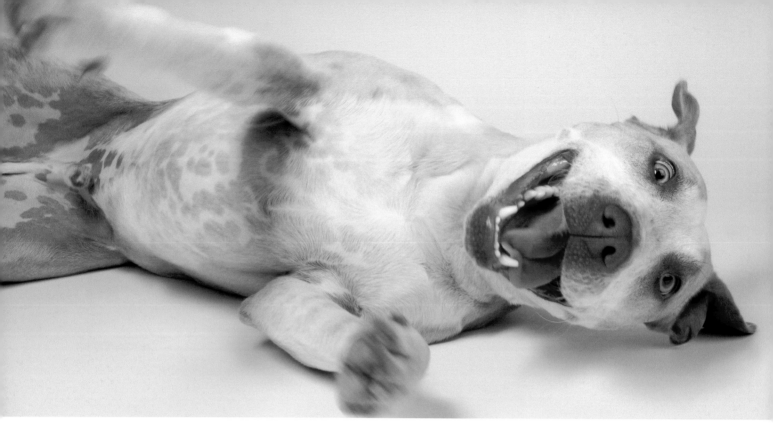

ECHO

CALIFORNIA
ECHO'S HOME HAS TWO OTHER DOGS, A CAT, A HORSE & 12 CHICKENS; EVERYONE GETS ALONG HAPPILY
AKA FUN GAME (BECAUSE JUST ABOUT EVERYTHING IS FUN TO ECHO...EXCEPT BATHTIME)
ADOPTED FROM MENDOCINO COAST HUMANE SOCIETY (MCHS)

Echo was born in a high-kill shelter. His mother belonged to a homeless man. When he was arrested, she was impounded and, a day later, delivered seven healthy pups. They were then placed in foster care through MCHS. Echo was adopted; however, after his new family discovered he was deaf, they quickly returned him. At that point, all of his siblings had been adopted, but Echo was still waiting for a home. Crissy Tadlock had been looking specifically for a pit bull, and once she met happy Echo, she knew he was the one. In the short time he has been with her family, Echo has earned his Canine Good Citizen certificate, graduated from two advanced obedience classes and learned over 30 hand signals. Echo also gives demos, participates in parades and competes in canine disc, where he has placed second and third in the Novice Division. Echo's deafness has never slowed him down. He has converted people who were afraid of pit bulls and educated people about deaf dogs. Crissy said, "Hopefully, people who have a negative opinion of pit bulls will see him at a competition and maybe think a little more. He's changed our lives too...Every opportunity we get to show someone... what a rescued, deaf pit bull is capable of, we take." Since adopting him, Crissy has started fostering pit bulls; Echo befriends them, acts like their big "brother" and shares his bed. He is protective of their chickens, too. One night, the chicks did not get locked up, and Crissy did not realize it. Echo found them in the dark and alerted Crissy as to where they were so she could get them safely inside.

34

DR. JACKSON

UTAH

HE IS ALWAYS IN THE WINDOW WAITING FOR ANNE WHEN SHE COMES HOME FROM WORK
AKA FERDINAND (AFTER THE BULL THAT DID NOT WANT TO FIGHT)
ADOPTED FROM THE UNIVERSITY OF UTAH MEDICAL CENTER DOG LABORATORY

When Dr. Jackson was about 2 years old, the dog laboratory at the University of Utah Medical Center pulled him from a local shelter, where he most likely would have been put down. He was used for 18 months in the lab as a practice dog for medical residents who were learning to do bronchoscopy; the residents looked at the lungs and trachea through an endoscope with the dog under general anesthesia. He was scoped once a month, lived in a kennel with his own run, was walked by volunteers and was adopted out after a year (but it took him longer to get adopted, probably because of his "breed"). Anne Vinsel, who works at the hospital, saw him at an adoption event and fell in love. She picked him because of his smarts, and because he is very visual and so is she (she is a painter and surgical photographer). Dr. Jackson is missing four teeth, which were cracked during the procedures at the lab. He now lives a very spoiled life on two floors of a Victorian house, has dog friends and visits dog parks. One of his former caretakers at the lab also walks him in the middle of the day while Anne is at work. He has his own couch, a window ottoman and a memory-foam dog bed. He enjoys all kinds of games and has created his own running track in Anne's painting studio. He loves all people, anything edible, tug of war, running up and down stairs, rolling in the grass and belly rubs.

RUMMY

WASHINGTON, DC
RUMMY IS A SPECIAL DOG—HE KNOWS THREE COMMANDS: SIT; LIE DOWN & HIGH FIVE
ADOPTED FROM A RESCUE THAT WAS FORCED TO CLOSE DUE TO HOARDING

Rummy was from the same litter as his sister Kuma (*see pgs. 44 & 45*), but their paths took very different turns. When Bobbie Jo Kite & Matthew Malzkuhn went to the rescue to adopt one of the puppies, Rummy was already taken, and so they adopted Kuma. Fast forward 10 months...the rescue contacted Bobbie Jo to see whether she could foster Rummy for two weeks. (His owners had been evicted, and had left him untrained, not housebroken, and with bleach added to his water bowl. The rescue had rushed Rummy to the vet to treat him.) When Rummy arrived at Bobbie Jo & Matt's, he was wild, unsocialized and proceeded to pee on their legs. Because Kuma loved him the instant he burst through the door, they agreed—two weeks, then Rummy would be gone. The two weeks were the longest weeks of their lives. He had clearly been the victim of terrible psychological and emotional abuse at his previous home. Rummy destroyed things, could not be walked, and peed out of submission. However, once the two weeks were up, they realized they could not let him go. They kept him, had him neutered and enrolled him in obedience class. It took him three months to comprehend the command "sit." After three years, Rummy now does not destroy items when left alone. He is still nervous around new people. It has been a long road, but they are rewarded with Rummy's devotion. Bobbie Jo said, "When he does love, he loves wholly and deeply."

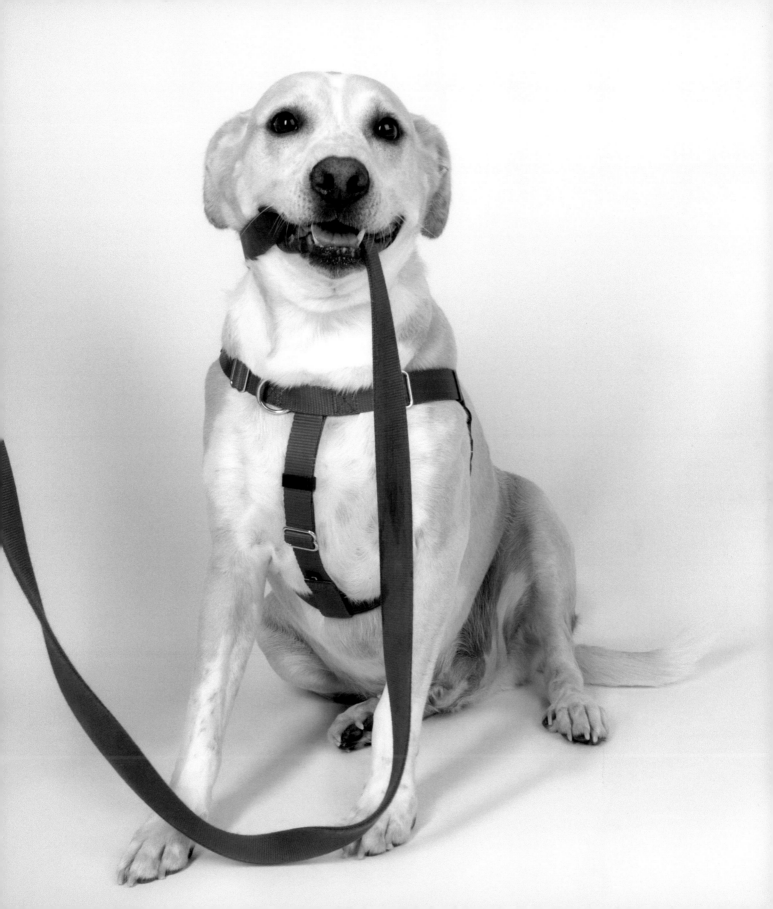

ELLIE MAE

ILLINOIS
LOVING & SWEET, ELLIE MAE ADORES KIDS, & LOVES TO HERD THE COUPLE'S TWIN BOYS
AKA MOOSE & ROAD BLOCK
ADOPTED FROM SECONDHAND SNOOTS RESCUE (SSR)

Found as a stray in Indiana and brought in to animal control, Ellie Mae was filthy, had collar marks on her neck and had obviously borne multiple litters. She may have been a backyard breeder dog whose puppies were taken from her. Ellie Mae was pulled by SSR just 30 minutes before she was scheduled to be euthanized. She was fostered by a great family, but, once, when she saw her foster dad taking off his belt, she ran off terrified with her tail between her legs. She then went to live with SSR's vice chairperson, Erica Brown, & her husband, Russell. They fell in love with her. Ellie Mae is slowly adjusting to life in the real world. She is afraid of many things. It takes time for her to warm up to new people, but she is learning that no one is going to hurt her ever again. Her family often takes her places so she can become better socialized. She is learning "how to be a dog." Ellie Mae has a number of health issues, too, including a sensitive stomach, pancreatitis that flares up when she gets stressed out, and possible lung damage since she coughs and wheezes and had walking pneumonia last winter. She is a sweet and loving girl who adores her family and enjoys having fun, such as leaping into the air when she gets "the zoomies." They hope she will earn her Canine Good Citizen and therapy dog certifications one day so she can help educate people about pit bulls.

RUBY

NEW JERSEY
A DADDY'S GIRL WHO DROOLS AT MEALTIMES, SLEEPS WITH A PILLOW & LOVES TO CUDDLE
AKA BOOPS
ADOPTED FROM A RESCUE THAT IS NO LONGER IN EXISTENCE

Found as a stray on the streets of Miami, Ruby was transported to the Philadelphia area by a rescue, where she remained for nearly a year. Tony & Jaque Russo found her online and fell in love with her. There are a lot of unanswered questions about her past, though. She was only 1.5 years old when they adopted her; she had been a stray and then had lived in a kennel at the rescue. However, when she first was adopted, she knew some commands and was already housetrained, even tapping her nose on the doorknob when she needed to go outside. She also had urine burns on her skin, and she was very thin. They were told she was microchipped, but she was not. Tony & Jaque were very disturbed to learn of charges that were later filed against the rescue, but some things about Ruby then started to make sense. However, the Russos remain grateful to everyone who helped save her. Fortunately, Ruby had no trouble adapting to her new home. She ran straight for her bed and toys and then jumped right into Jaque's lap. She knew she had come home. The Russos were initially nervous about adopting a large pit bull, but that all changed once Ruby arrived. Tony said, "We attend every positive pit bull event we can, wearing our "Team Sarge" (*see pgs. 130 & 131*) T-shirts. Ruby wears her bandana and anti-BSL pins....She's goofier than any other dog we've had...but she's a dog, just the same as any other..."

KUMA

WASHINGTON, DC
KUMA LOVES BALLOONS & WILL PAW AT THEM UNTIL THEY POP
ADOPTED FROM A RESCUE THAT WAS FORCED TO CLOSE DUE TO HOARDING

Kuma was born to a young pit bull whose owners left her tied outside in their yard because they did not want a deaf dog. Neighbors fed the dog for three months before deciding to report the situation to animal control, which then surrendered the mom and her litter to a rescue. However, the conditions at the rescue were not good. When Bobbie Jo Kite & Matthew Malzkuhn went to look at the puppies, they found Kuma had mange and an eye infection, and was covered in her own urine. Despite her situation, she was already a feisty little pup. It was Matt who wanted a pit bull puppy. Bobbie Jo did not set out to adopt one, but she fell in love with Kuma. Kuma opened her eyes to the plight of pit bulls, and because of her, Bobbie Jo has done volunteer work with pit bulls in many parts of the country. Under Matt & Bobbie Jo's care, Kuma enrolled in puppy kindergarten and grew to be a healthy 68-lb. dog. She is now extremely loved by many for her antics. Kuma is hearing, but Matt & Bobbie Jo are both deaf. Kuma is their service dog. She lets them know when someone is at the door by standing by the door and barking. She also paws at them to get their attention. Kuma knows commands in sign language. She likes to play with her brother Rummy (see pgs. 38 & 39) and to go for walks. Every time Kuma sees someone walking toward her, she wags her tail and gets a goofy grin on her big head. If the person pets her for even just two seconds, that will make her whole day.

ALAN

TEXAS

KNOWN AROUND THE SHELTER AS A HUGGER, HE LOVES TO WRAP HIS ARMS AROUND YOU & CUDDLE
UP FOR ADOPTION AT AUSTIN HUMANE SOCIETY (AHS)

In July 2009, the HSUS, the Humane Society of Missouri, and the ASPCA raided multiple dog fighting operations in eight states on one day. It became the largest single day of actions against dog fighting in U.S. history. Dogs were seized from properties that day and held in isolation in various boarding facilities around the country until the trials concluded...a year and a half later. Alan's mother had been seized that day and gave birth to Alan while she was in confinement at a boarding facility in northern Texas that was housing some of the dogs from the bust. After the holding period was over, Alan was relinquished to AHS. Alan suffers from a non-contagious, extremely treatable skin condition as a result of the stress he has experienced in his short life. Alan has never met a stranger. He immediately friends and solicits petting from everyone he meets. People melt when he looks at them with his longing eyes and brilliant smile. Alan has spent all of his life in a shelter environment, and, as a result, he shows signs of anxiety and stress when leaving the shelter. The world is a brand new place for him to experience—and it is overwhelming. While at AHS, staff and volunteers have been working with him to help him learn how wonderful the world is. He is slowly making progress. A little shy at first, he becomes quickly attached and trusting. He is a bundle of love. At the time this book went to print, Alan was still up for adoption at AHS.

XENA

TEXAS
XENA DOES THE BEST FULL-BODY WIGGLE EVER WHEN SHE IS EXCITED
UP FOR ADOPTION AT AUSTIN HUMANE SOCIETY (AHS)

In July 2009, Xena was seized from a suspected dog fighter during the same multistate raids that seized Alan's mother (*see pg. 46*). She was housed in a boarding facility in northern Texas for 18 months, and held as evidence until the trial concluded and her abusers were prosecuted. After the holding period was over, she was relinquished to AHS. Xena's ears were butchered so close she has almost no external ears at all, and her tail was docked at an unusual length. All that is known about Xena's history is that she was used for breeding and that she had had multiple litters while she was at the dog fighting operation. Xena does struggle to overcome her past. She is sometimes fearful and mistrusting of other dogs, and is also uncertain around children, since she has not met very many in her life. However, she has grown to love people. Every day she makes progress. She is friendly and eager to please, and she will do anything for squeaky toys, which she thinks are better than any treat. At the time this book went to print, Xena was still up for adoption at AHS.

47

JASMINE

UTAH
PEOPLE FALL IN LOVE WITH THIS FUNNY, PLAYFUL "POCKET PITTIE", WHO WADDLES WHEN SHE WALKS
AKA PIPSQUEAK
ADOPTED FROM BEST FRIENDS ANIMAL SOCIETY (BFAS)

When the HSUS's animal fighting team worked alongside the Jefferson County Humane Society in southeast Ohio to rescue 200 dogs from a suspected dog fighting operation in 2010, it was the largest single dog fighting yard that the HSUS had ever uncovered. These dogs came to be known as the "Ohio 200." Jasmine was one of those dogs. She was 25 lbs. and had some scarring, and so it is possible that she could have been fought or used as a bait dog when she was still a puppy. Traci Madson, who adopted Jasmine from BFAS, named her after Sweet Jasmine, a Vick dog who died shortly after being rescued. Jasmine now lives with two other dogs (see pgs. 107, 142 & 143), who adore her. For the first week, every time Traci would reach out to pet her, Jasmine would shy away like she thought she was going to be hit. She will come when called but will keep her distance and at times will run away or back up if someone reaches out toward her. Most of the Ohio 200 were chained outside to wheel axles with no shelter. So Jasmine has learned to observe the other dogs to figure out from them what she should do at Traci's house. Traci has only had her a few months, but Jasmine is already working toward her Canine Good Citizen certificate. Since Jasmine is so affectionate, eager to please and energetic, Traci thinks she would do well in agility and as a therapy dog.

BETSY

RHODE ISLAND
SWEET 75-LB. BETSY THINKS SHE IS A LAPDOG
AKA BETS, BIG SLOPPY, SLOPSTER & BIG MAMA
ADOPTED FROM HANDSOME DAN'S RESCUE (HDR)

Heather Gutshall (see pg. 146) of HDR had posted some photos of Betsy on the HDR Facebook page, and the look on Betsy's face and her big, sad eyes instantly melted Deanna Casanovas. Two-year-old Betsy most likely had been a "throwaway mama." Her ears were clipped at home unevenly with scissors and never sutured, so they probably bled until she healed herself. Given her yellow belly from sleeping in her own urine and her infected eyes and paws, it is believed that Betsy was kept in a crate for most of her life. Heather pulled Betsy from Providence Animal Care & Control. Deanna adopted her, and she moved into Deanna's home with her boyfriend Patrick King and their other dog Gozer, (see pg. 122). Now Betsy loves life. She likes to swim. She loves all other dogs and is Ms. Popularity at the dog park, where small dogs climb all over her. Betsy has a maternal instinct with the couple's cats. Most people walk right up to her sweet, goofy face; others cross the street. However, Betsy loves all people and children and will lick them ceaselessly. She needs to sit on whoever is closest to her—she sits on Gozer while he naps. Sometimes in the evening when everyone is relaxing, she will roll off the couch right onto the floor without batting an eye. If she is sleepy, which is often, and someone rubs her head while she is sitting on the floor, she will fall asleep right there, sitting up. Deanna said of her dogs, "I am surrounded by love, cuteness and sloppiness and all things great!"

49

LILY

MARYLAND
LILY JUMPED A 6-FT. FENCE TO CHASE SQUIRRELS...SHE IS NOW IN TRAINING TO CURB HER ENTHUSIASM
AKA LILY WONDERDOG (FORMERLY KNOWN AS LOLLIE WONDERDOG)
ADOPTED FROM MONTGOMERY COUNTY HUMANE SOCIETY (MCHS)

Animal control responded to a call about a dog left to die, thrown away in a garbage dumpster. When the officers responded, they opened the dumpster and found Lily, covered in scars, scrapes and cuts. She had been bred repeatedly and was very skinny and in bad shape. Despite suffering abuse at someone's hands, she was not afraid of her rescuers and licked them. She was brought into the shelter, where she quickly earned the nickname "Wonderdog." Pit bull type dogs were not normally allowed to be fostered out because the shelter thought they were "too risky;" however, Lily's wonderful nature changed that. She was allowed to be fostered, and now there are many pit bull type dogs in the MCHS foster program. Lily's foster "mom" nursed her back to health and posted Lily on her blog, "Love and a Six-foot Leash," which is how Jennifer Mills & John McGlorthan found her. Sweet Lily greeted them with rounds of licking. Lily has definitely been an "ambassadog." Jennifer's mother shrieked, "A PIT BULL! WITH MY GRANDKIDS!" when she was told they were adopting Lily, but now she is in love with her new "granddog." The couple's children adore Lily, and their friends who once thought they were crazy for bringing a "vicious pit bull" home to a family with small children are now all enchanted by her. Jennifer said, "Hopefully with Lily's help, we can get more families to get these pits out of the shelters and into loving homes where they belong."

ZAPP

NEVADA
A BEAUTIFUL, ACTIVE GIRL WHO IS EAGER TO PLEASE
RESCUED FROM EUTHANASIA AT A VETERINARY CLINIC

Zapp had been dumped by her previous owners and picked up by a rescue group in Detroit. The rescue group brought Zapp into a veterinary clinic to be euthanized due to a major parvo outbreak in the area. (To help deal with this crisis, many clinics were providing free euthanasia.) Veronica Selco knew a friend's mother who worked at the clinic. Her friend's mother fell in love with Zapp, kept her from being euthanized and brought her home. Months later, Zapp ended up in Las Vegas with Veronica and what she calls her "Bully Brigade" (*see pgs. 94, 95, 100 & 101*). Zapp is a beautiful and active girl who is truly living *la dolce vita* in her new home. She enjoys the best food possible, gets tons of exercise and training and has many "siblings" to play with. She competes in DockDogs, weight pulling, flyball and sprint racing. Zapp enjoys tug, fetch, swimming and working for food. She also loves her Jolly Pets ball. Veronica needed to buy her a zoo-rated Jolly Pets ball (one strong enough for tigers!) after Zapp ate through the one designed for dogs. Playful Zapp loves to wrestle with her "siblings" but also loves downtime, too, especially cuddling with Veronica & her husband, Scott.

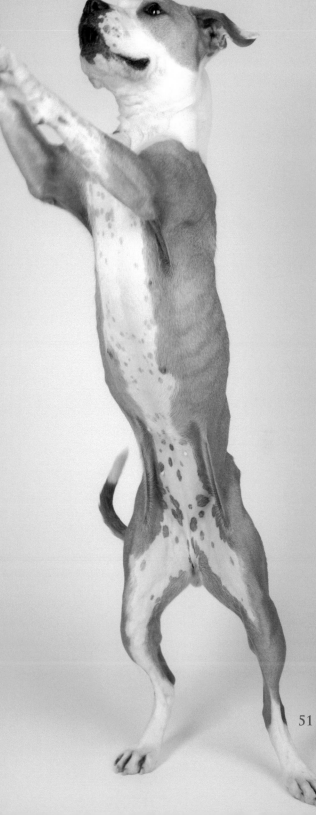

51

BRUNO

NEW YORK
SENSITIVE, QUIET & WELL-MANNERED, THIS 60-LB. LAPDOG LOVES TO SNUGGLE
AKA BRUNO-BOY
ADOPTED FROM ANIMAL CARE & CONTROL OF NYC, MANHATTAN (AC&CNY)

Bruno was found collarless on 107th Street in Queens, just lying injured on the sidewalk. He was extremely malnourished and underweight. His report says he was "dull, depressed, lethargic, recumbent and falling down." He had been hit by a car and had difficulty breathing. Within a day, his appetite picked up; however, he contracted kennel cough and was scheduled to be put down. Jessica Mawhirt & Charles More had been following the dogs that were in the "To Be Destroyed" folder for AC&CNY's Facebook page. What caught her attention was "the most amazing memo" written by one of the shelter's volunteers about Bruno:

> There is nothing, not one thing, that isn't completely, crazily lovable about this extraordinary dog. He has hearts drawn on his kennel card! Everyone, men and women alike, swoon over this 2 year old. "What a beautiful dog!" said one vet tech walking by, who then of course had to stop and pet him...he is THAT impossible to resist. Our beloved Bruno, who adores other dogs and is the diplomat of his ward, eliciting kisses from all the other dogs through the bars...is quickly running out of time...which makes us absolutely crazy with sadness. Bruno, who...loves to snuggle and curl up and give kisses and just hang out...could be a diplomat in the world, not just his ward. PLEASE, don't let this extraordinary dog down. He is one of those pups who will change the lives of everyone around him with his love, generosity and noble spirit."

Jessica said, "He did change my life...he has completed our family (see pgs. 56 & 57)...we are so happy we found him."

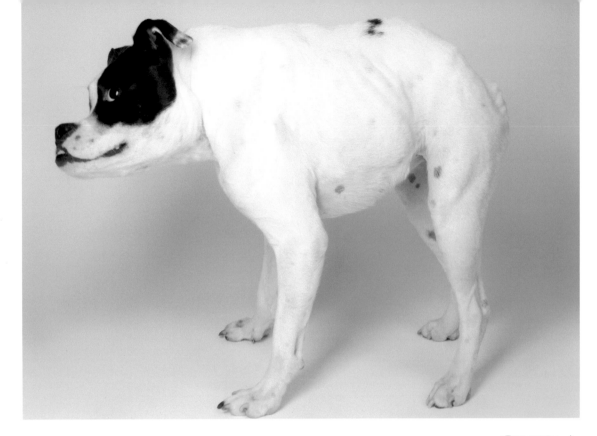

CUDA

NORTH CAROLINA

PEOPLE ARE DRAWN TO CUDA, WHO STEALS THE HEART OF EVERYONE SHE MEETS
CUDA WAS GIVEN TO THEM BY HER PREVIOUS "OWNERS"

A couple at a gas station approached Julie LeRoy; they were looking to rehome a pit bull. Julie took one look at the dog and knew she had to take her. Julie & her husband, Scott, knew nothing about Cuda's past; however, Cuda has physical traits associated with inbreeding, including cow-hocked rear legs, an undersized body, a malformed jaw with a massive underbite, a curved spine including fused vertebrae in her neck and tail, asymmetrical ears and feet, an enlarged heart and an underdeveloped pancreas, resulting in the early onset of diabetes. She is in no physical pain but visits the vet twice monthly to monitor her diabetes and to make sure other issues have not developed. After Julie created a Facebook page for Cuda, the couple who gave Cuda to Julie resurfaced to tell her Cuda's story. They had bought Cuda from a breeder on Craigslist. He would not let them into his house but brought the puppies out to them. Cuda was held off to the side. The couple felt sorry for her and paid $50 for her. Julie feels 100 percent certain that Cuda's condition was caused by inbreeding. Julie & Scott are in the process of creating "Cuda's Law," which focuses on breeder regulations, including certification based on educational classes, inspection, litter fees, spay/neuter requirements for any dog on the property not being used to breed, and more stringent medical exams. Cuda goes to events to educate people about backyard and irresponsible breeders and to promote pet adoption. She has helped raise money for rescue with her appearances through kissing booths, T-shirt sales and even paintings she has created. She teaches people about pit bulls and teaches children about accepting people as they are and not letting differences keep them from befriending those who are different from them. When people see Cuda for the first time, they have stunned expressions that turn into broad smiles. She steals the heart of everyone she meets.

WINNIE

NEW YORK
A CROWD PLEASER & TOTAL HAM, WINNIE LOVES KIDS & MAKES FRIENDS WHEREVER SHE GOES
AKA WIN, WINNIE-MA-JIG, WINNIE BEAR & QUEEN OF THE HOUSE
ADOPTED FROM ANIMAL HAVEN (AH)

Jessica Mawhirt & Charles More had just graduated from college and wanted to adopt an older dog because they wanted a calm, gentle soul in their household. Enter Winnie—the exact opposite. As a puppy, Winnie was brought from a high-kill shelter in Georgia to New York City's AH. When the couple visited the rescue, Winnie greeted them by rolling over onto their feet and wagging her tail rapidly. They were so smitten with her that any thoughts of an older dog went right out the window. They put in an application for her that day. A total character and joy, Winnie entertains the couple by staying perched in her armchair all day to look out the window and keep an eye on things, acting as the couple's morning alarm clock, flopping down to succumb to her laziness mid-walk, and swimming and chasing animals on their trips to the Thousand Islands. Since adopting Winnie, they are completely invested in animal rescue, and their eyes have been opened to the plight of pit bull type dogs. Jessica even started a blog about Winnie and her "brother," Bruno (*see pgs. 52 & 53*) to help open people's hearts to these dogs. Both of the couple's families would never have considered even approaching a pit bull type dog on the street, but after spending time with Winnie & Bruno, they have come around. Jessica's father now calls Winnie & Bruno the best two dogs in the world.

56

FINNIGAN
PENNSYLVANIA
CANNOT CONTROL HIS "LICKER" WHEN HE IS WITH BABIES & PUPPIES (HE LOVES TO KISS THEM)
AKA FINN, FINNY, FINN-DOG & BE-BOP
ADOPTED FROM OPEN ARMS RESQ & REFURRAL (OAR&R)

Finnigan started out his life in a Virginia puppy mill. He was fortunate enough to be rescued and transported to Open Arms ResQ in Pennsylvania. Kelley Simon was searching online for a Great Dane to rescue, and Finn's profile came up. When she went to meet him at his foster home, he gave her lots of kisses, and she knew he was going to be a great dog. Inquisitive and attentive Finn, an immediate stand out in his puppy kindergarten class, learned quickly and was eager to please. Since being adopted at 4 months old, Finn has shared his home with numerous foster dogs, whom he helped welcome into the home, including a female Mastiff, and Kelley's "failed foster" Gideon, his Great Dane "brother." The two are now inseparable. Finn plays big "brother," showing Gideon the rules of the house and calming Gideon's anxious behavior. Kelley lives an active lifestyle, and along the way, Finn has been by her side. He loves riding in cars, playing fetch, destuffing stuffed toys, catching frisbees and meeting people. He's a crowd pleaser, especially at the many "meet & greets" Kelley does for Mid-Atlantic Great Dane Rescue League. Finn is a well-rounded, happy and goofy dog. He dispels everyone's fear about pit bulls; he is the perfect example of a well-socialized pup.

59

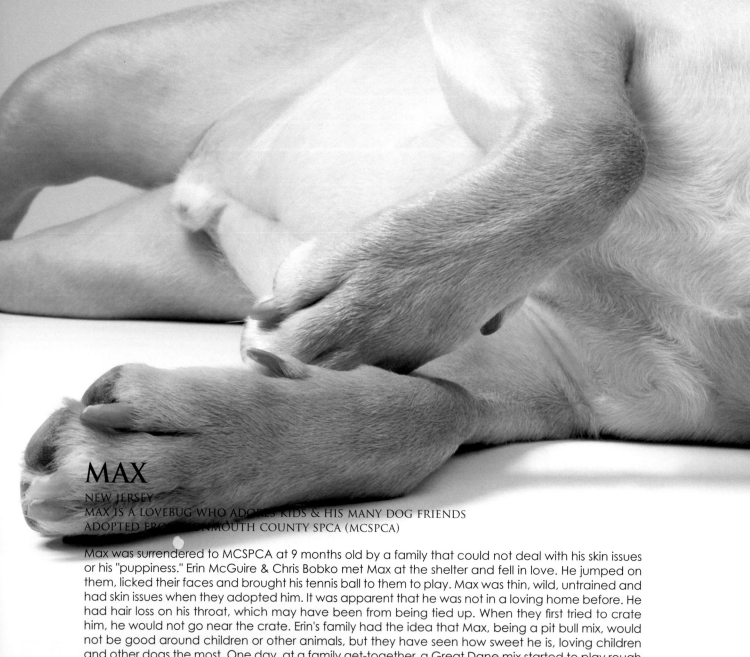

MAX
NEW JERSEY
MAX IS A LOVEBUG WHO ADORES KIDS & HIS MANY DOG FRIENDS
ADOPTED FROM MONMOUTH COUNTY SPCA (MCSPCA)

Max was surrendered to MCSPCA at 9 months old by a family that could not deal with his skin issues or his "puppiness." Erin McGuire & Chris Bobko met Max at the shelter and fell in love. He jumped on them, licked their faces and brought his tennis ball to them to play. Max was thin, wild, untrained and had skin issues when they adopted him. It was apparent that he was not in a loving home before. He had hair loss on his throat, which may have been from being tied up. When they first tried to crate him, he would not go near the crate. Erin's family had the idea that Max, being a pit bull mix, would not be good around children or other animals, but they have seen how sweet he is, loving children and other dogs the most. One day, at a family get-together, a Great Dane mix started to play rough with a Pug, who is Max's closest "cousin." The Pug was repeatedly getting knocked down, but the Great Dane mix persisted. Max ran over, stood over the Pug to protect her, and barked at the Great Dane mix to say enough was enough. Max attends many events through the Underdogs group (*see pgs. 70 & 71*) to teach people about pit bulls. Now that he has had training, gets regular exercise and is in the right home, he is mellow and has a calming way about him. Erin said, "It was obvious that Max wanted to please us, and all it took was giving him love back. Not only did we change Max's life, but he changed ours as well. He has become a part of our family and makes us happy every day."

60

CARLA LOU

NEW JERSEY
LOVES PEOPLE, KIDS & OTHER DOGS, & "EMITS RAYS OF SUNSHINE" WHEREVER SHE GOES
AKA LOULABELLE, MOOKIE SUZUKI, MOOKIE SUE, SOOKIE MANX & MONKEY SUE
ADOPTED FROM CHAKO PIT BULL RESCUE (CHAKO)

The four-legged founder of Pinups for Pitbulls (PFPB), wonderful Carla Lou is a true ambassador for pit bull type dogs and, at 17-years-young, for elderbulls, too. A star in her own right, Carla Lou has helped "mom" Deirdre "Little Darling" Franklin win first place in *The American Dog Magazine*'s contest for "Voice Against Illegal Dogfighting," and has been featured in magazines, newspapers, and more—simply google the words "Carla Lou" and you will see. However, Carla Lou's start in life was not so auspicious. Abandoned and left for dead in a Texas basement at 1 year old, covered in mange, and scared for her life, she was alone for days before someone found her. It took Deirdre a month to gain the trust of Chako so she could have Carla Lou sent across the country to her for adoption. Carla Lou was skittish for about a year afterward; however, she loved and trusted Deirdre from the moment they met. She blossomed quickly into a wonderful dog. She has been by Deirdre's side in numerous cities and towns for the last 16 years. She has traveled to photo shoots and attended PFPB events all over the country. And she's a survivor. She has won her battles against blindness, loss of hearing, cancer, Lyme disease and discrimination (some schools denied her as a humane educator because of her "breed"). It was keeping Carla Lou and other shelter dogs like her safe from breed ban laws and discrimination that was Deirdre's inspiration for starting PFPB in the first place. Deirdre said, "She is a constant influence for changing minds and hearts. She is the love of my life."

BAXTER BEAN

NEW JERSEY
LOVES STARRING WITH "SISTER" CARLA LOU IN "MOM'S" PINUPS FOR PITBULLS CALENDARS
AKA BAXTER BEANERTON, BABY MAN, BABY SONGS & SONGS
ADOPTED FROM PET RESCUE OF MERCER (PRM)

Baxter Bean, along with his littermates, was dropped off at PetSmart in Hamilton, NJ for PRM to deal with. The 5-month-old puppies all were dying of parvo, and Baxter had been burned with a caustic chemical that dripped down his hips and spine and caused nerve damage. Believed to be backyard breeders, the family who had dumped the puppies and abused Baxter, was found. The owner claimed Baxter's burns were not burns at all but were scars that had happened when Baxter "crawled under the fence." Even though you can see the actual places the drips burned him, the city of Trenton never pursued the case. After Deirdre Franklin & Jeffrey Loncosky fostered and then adopted him, Baxter was very sad and had low energy for the whole next year. He would not play at all. Instead, he lay on the couch and seemed to mope and wallow. His "brother" Howie and his "sister" Carla Lou helped him come out of his shell little by little. Although he will always have visible scars down his back from the chemical burns, his emotional scars seem to have healed. He is now wildly excited about simple pleasures. He likes to snuggle, give kisses, and watch movies. He likes long walks, short drives (he throws up on long ones) and loves to lie with his "sister" (possible girlfriend?) Zoe Michelle. He is very social and has "the life." Surrounded by loving friends, both human and dog, he enjoys learning how to swim, to do agility and to do anything fun. He can even run obstacle courses, and he knows how to jump through hoops (hula hoops!).

BRANDO

NEW JERSEY
SOON TO BE ENTERING THE WORLD'S LONGEST TONGUE COMPETITION
ADOPTED FROM THE ANIMAL ORPHANAGE (TAO)

Brando was found tied to a tree out in the middle of the woods. He was brought into TAO, vetted, neutered and put up for adoption. He was only there for two weeks before Denise D'Antonio saw him and knew he was the dog for her. Brando now lives with Denise and his Presa Canario/pit bull mix "brother," Brody (*see pgs. 72 & 73*). Brando loves to go for walks with Brody, as well as play tug in the backyard and sunbathe on the deck. Brando is a very happy-go-lucky dog. He loves people and other dogs. When he meets a dog he really likes, he pins his ears back and does what Denise calls his "pittie patter dance" of excitement with his front paws. When Denise adopted Brando, she was unaware of just how bad of a rap pit bull type dogs get. She said, "I don't think anyone understands it until you have one, and you hear comments directed at your dog." Brando is the reason Denise started volunteering for pit bull rescue and advocacy groups. She currently volunteers for two groups: Pit Bull Rescue Central and Lilo's Promise Animal Rescue. Brody and Brando both help to acclimate the many foster dogs that come into the home. When he sees people out on walks, he always wags his tail, and that makes him approachable in people's opinions. Denise said, "Other than the fact that some people look at them in a negative way, they're just like having any other dog."

64

RILEY

COLORADO

BEYOND SPOILED, SHE TRULY LIVES "THE LIFE OF RILEY"

AKA RILEY ROO, RI RI, LOVEBUG, SNUGGLES, LEE LEE, MONSTER, OTTER, LOVE & GIRLY GIRL

ADOPTED FROM HUMANE SOCIETY OF THE PIKES PEAK REGION (HSPPR)

Riley was found as a stray in Colorado Springs. She was skinny, but full of life and personality. Laura Kana originally went to the shelter looking at all the pups, and saw 11-month-old Riley wrestling with another puppy. She had just been brought in, so Laura put her name down. Once the holding period was up, her family adopted her and loaded her up in the car. She curled up between Laura and her sister in the backseat and fell asleep. Laura said, "I am forever grateful that I found my best friend that day." Riley is a fun little trickster and a fast learner. She has a fan club of people who love her to pieces. She loves people (and is completely drawn to children and babies) and will do anything for attention. She knows over 40 commands; her most unusual two are limping and wagging the tip of her tail on command. Being super fast, she has garnered many first-place finishes at agility trials and has four AKC agility titles (NAP, NJP, OAP and OJP). The dogs are a part of the family's life in the mountains, going hiking, camping, swimming and romping in the snow with them. Riley could not have it much better. Riley also lives with four cats, including Hazel, who is Riley's BFF. Riley entertains everyone with her favorite antics, such as squirrel patrol (taken seriously on the back deck); wrestling with her "brother," Homer; snuggling with Hazel; and swimming (she is not called "otter" for nothing).

BAZOOKA

NEW YORK
BAZOOKA IS EXTREMELY GENTLE WITH OTHER DOGS, PEOPLE & KIDS
FOUND AS A STRAY

James and a friend found Bazooka as a stray in the Bronx. He was just a couple of months old. James knew that Bazooka needed to be cared for. He needed food and water, a bath and a visit to the vet. James took him in, and Bazooka immediately became a part of his life. They have been by each other's side ever since. James will do anything for Bazooka. Bazooka has been living the good life for the past 9.5 years. He is so special to James & Vanessa; they could not imagine life without him. Even though he is almost 10 years old, he still plays like he is a puppy. James & Vanessa's friends often arrange for their pets to have playdates with Bazooka, who loves other dogs. Bazooka loves people, too—even those he meets for the first time. He is a cuddlebug, and is very sensitive to those around him. If Vanessa or James is having a bad day, he knows and will walk right up to them and kiss their faces. Vanessa & James are frequently entertained by Bazooka, who has so much personality it is as if he were human. In December 2010, James & Vanessa rescued another dog (*see pg. 69*), Nutella. She has become Bazooka's shadow. He has taken on the role of a big "brother" with her, always looking after her. Bazooka has helped change people's minds about pit bull type dogs, too; many people cannot believe how friendly and well-behaved he is.

NUTELLA

NEW YORK
SHE LOVES TO WATCH VANESSA COOK; SHE KNOWS SHE IS GOING TO GET SOME YUMMY TREATS
ADOPTED FROM ANIMAL HAVEN (AH)

Nutella was found roaming the streets of the Bronx. At the time, she was still a small puppy, and was in fairly bad shape. She had a large bite on her face, and her eye was swollen and infected. The person who found her brought her in to AH, where she was treated and nursed back to health. She is now 100 percent healthy. James & Vanessa adopted her. When they first brought her home, they could tell that she was very scared and was uncomfortable being touched. That all quickly changed. Now Nutella's purpose in life is to be loved and to give love. Nutella, more than anything in the world, loves to give kisses. No matter what you say to her or what you are doing, she will just look at you and lick your face. An incredibly sweet dog and true cuddlebug, Nutella enjoys snuggling, getting petted and being held. She was born to love. A very happy dog with a great deal of energy, too, Nutella is extremely playful and enjoys the company of other dogs, including her big "brother," Bazooka (see *pg. 68*), whom she follows all around the house. She, like Bazooka, is changing people's opinions of pit bull type dogs, too. Everyone loves her. She loves people, too, and always welcomes them with (you guessed it) lots of kisses.

LOLA

NEW JERSEY
A DOG LOVER AT HEART, LOLA LOVES TO (& LIVES TO) PLAY
ADOPTED FROM MONMOUTH COUNTY SPCA (MCSPCA)

Lola was brought into MCSPCA by someone who claimed he found her as a stray. However, she had stitches on her face from a dog bite. She was then adopted out twice, but returned both times. The last time she was returned, the adopters told the shelter that they thought she may be deaf. This did not stop Maggie Lazur and her husband from adopting her. They knew she was the dog for them. They communicate with Lola using hand signals. Lola knows over 20 hand signals at the moment and recently started taking agility lessons. Remarkably resourceful and smart, Lola has amazing dexterity and cognitive skills that have turned her into an "expert thief." She is able to open gates, latches, doors and even locks to get something that she wants to play with. She seems to be able to make a game or toy out of anything. If she is given a treat that excites her, she will throw it in the air with her mouth, play bow to it, hit it with her paw, and then chase it across the room while wagging her tail. Maggie's husband was unsure about adopting Lola because of her "breed." He is now crazy about her. Lola inspired Maggie to start the Monmouth County Underdogs, which focuses on changing public perceptions of pit bulls, fundraising for groups that rescue bully breeds and providing bully-breed owners with the opportunity for on-leash socializing. The couple has met so many great pit bulls through the Underdogs that it is hard for them to believe that they ever had a concern.

BRODY

NEW JERSEY
BRODY LOVES ALL PEOPLE
ADOPTED FROM STREET TAILS ANIMAL RESCUE (STAR)

Brody was found on the side of the road by a veterinary technician. She saw him lying there lifeless and thought he was dead. As she approached him, she noticed he was breathing but in bad shape. He was covered in ticks, and his ears were cropped, caked in dried blood and sutured using fishing line—likely a do-it-yourself crop job. She put him in her car and took him to work. The staff took great care of him. They cleaned him up and got him neutered and ready to be adopted out. The veterinary technician who found Brody decided to foster him through STAR. Later, Denise D'Antonio found Brody on Petfinder.com, and it was love at first sight. The next day he was home with Denise. Brody loves to go for walks and play fetch. One of the cutest things about Brody is that every morning is Christmas to him—he wakes up so happy! He runs over to his "brother" Brando (see pg. 64 & 65) and licks his muzzle until he wakes up. Of course, Denise gets a free "Brody bath" too. Denise always gets compliments when she is out walking him because he walks so well on leash. Some people are afraid of him because of his size, "breed" and his cropped ears. Others are curious and ask what breed he is or ask to pet him. He loves to sleep on the bed, sunbathe on the deck, go for walks and, in the summer, he loves to go swimming at his "grandmother's" house. Denise said, "The past is behind him. Although he may have some physical scars showing, luckily he can't see them."

BLAZE

MARYLAND
EVERYONE WHO MEETS BLAZE FALLS IN LOVE WITH HIM
AKA BLIZZARD, SPARKY, TAZ, POODLE, BLAZENSTEIN, B-MAN, MONSTER, LANGOLIER & STUD
FOUND AS A STRAY

A friend of Shanley Crutchfield found a young dog, who was shivering from the cold and rain, emaciated and near death under a bridge in Philadelphia. Shanley adopted him, and to this day, if she wants Blaze to go outside in the rain, she has to pick him up and carry him out. When she first got Blaze, he was malnourished and very ill. Shanley quickly nursed him back to health. She believes he is a victim of the world of dog fighting due to his scars and dog aggression. Her parents, David & Jean Marie Crutchfield, were not sold on the idea of a pit bull, but Blaze soon won them over and now they adore him. Once he got settled into his new home, his life changed overnight. He is a member of the family and now spends his days lounging on couches. Blaze alternates weeks between Shanley's home and her parents' home, where he lies poolside on a chaise lounge and goes on hikes. Their old dog, Angel, was his only canine friend, but she had to be put down, and he has only had people friends since. He loves people and playing with his stuffed toys, rope and soccer ball. Blaze has had many health issues. Shanley said, "He is the most high maintenance dog anyone in my family has had...But there isn't a day that his love doesn't make it all worth it." She added, "I have his portrait tattooed on my leg. Some people wear their heart on their sleeve. Mine is on my calf."

THUMPER

TEXAS
A VERY VISUAL DOG, THUMPER WATCHES BIRDS IN THE YARD & BASKETBALL ON TV
ADOPTED FROM AUSTIN PETS ALIVE (APA)

Thumper was born hearing but became deaf as a result of antibiotics used to save her from parvo when she was 5 months old. Bobby Loeffler & Summer Crider had wanted a dog for five years, but they were waiting for fate to deliver the dog to them. Once they found a house with a big backyard, they looked around for a dog to join them. Their friend, who was temporarily fostering Thumper, posted her on Facebook. She then brought Thumper over to Summer & Bobby's house for dinner, and they instantly fell in love with her. Thumper joined them one week later. Thumper is now very healthy. They named her "Thumper" because the only way they could call her was if they thumped their feet on the ground so she could feel the vibrations. Summer is deaf, too, and so the couple communicate with Thumper using American Sign Language. Thumper picked up signs quickly and now knows over 30 commands. She is a very visually dependent dog (her foster family communicated with her by flashlight). Thumper has become the focus of the couple's lives. They spoil her, and she has been the happiest dog they have ever seen. Thumper is great with people but is obsessed with other dogs, almost preferring to wrestle and play with them than to hang out with people. She even barks when she sees dogs on television. Thumper and her deaf dog friend Rimel are identical when it comes to eating, sleeping, walking and getting attention.

RIMEL

TEXAS
EVERYBODY'S SWEETHEART—RIMEL LOVES GETTING ATTENTION
ADOPTED FROM TOWN LAKE ANIMAL CENTER

When Rimel was found as a stray and brought to the shelter where Mickie Brunton volunteered, he was less than 1 year old and was very sick with an upper respiratory infection. Vets suspect the infection may have caused his deafness. He was already neutered, so he most likely had an owner at some point. Mickie fell in love with his personality and tried to find him a permanent home. However, after a week, she adopted him herself. Mickie, who is also deaf, trained Rimel using American Sign Language, and he learned five signs the first week she brought him home. He uses his snout and paws to get Mickie's attention. Now he knows too many signs to count. He is taking advanced classes, and Mickie hopes he will earn his Canine Good Citizen certificate this year. He is able to be walked leash-free, and he knows to glance at the person he is with, at times, in case his attention is needed. When Mickie signs "hug," he gently stands with his front paws on her hips and allows her to hug him. When she signs "get him," he walks over to the nearest person and, using his snout or paws, gets the person's attention and walks back to her. The importance Mickie placed on his regimen and training have paid off tenfold. He is now one confident and obedient dog who loves people and other dogs and is amazing with kids, even letting Mickie's young nieces and nephews sit on him to pet him. Rimel is a great ambassador for pit bull type dogs and deaf dogs, too.

SHELBY

SHELBY'S STORY IS TOLD IN THE BOOK—SHELBY'S GRACE: FROM ABUSED PUP TO ANGEL OF MERCY
ADOPTED FROM BLOOMFIELD ANIMAL SHELTER (BAS)

Shelby was named for the Shell gas station where someone had left her tied outside for two days in the cold winter of 2008. She was eventually taken to BAS, where Joe Dwyer, Jr. was a volunteer. Shelby was depressed at the shelter and did not want to eat or go for walks. Joe quickly became attached to her and felt that if he did not adopt her soon, she would die at the shelter. Joe and his wife think Shelby was possibly used as a bait dog or was a victim of cruelty because of the injuries she had to her back legs when they adopted her. After recovering from surgery, Shelby's sadness lifted, and she found her niche: Shelby has a talent for making people feel happy and loved, so Joe had her certified as a therapy dog. Even though Shelby is great with all dogs and people, she was denied access to two facilities looking for a therapy dog because of her "breed." Joe & Shelby did not let that hold them back. Shelby has since visited schools, senior-citizen homes and juvenile detention centers, and has acted as a bereavement dog. In spite of her history of abuse, Shelby has nothing but kindness to give to everyone she meets. Inspired by Shelby's story, Joe wrote the book *Shelby's Grace*, and, as a motivational speaker, Joe brings Shelby with him to his talks about everything from compassion for animals to bullying. At his speaking engagements and on her therapy-dog visits, Joe & Shelby work together to change people's opinions of pit bulls and pit bull type dogs.

MONKEY BUSINESS

NEW YORK
CHARMING MONKEY BUSINESS MAKES FRIENDS WHEREVER SHE GOES
AKA MONKEY & MONKEY B
UP FOR ADOPTION AT ANIMAL FARM FOUNDATION (AFF)

Seized from an alleged dogfighter in New York, 4-year-old Monkey Business was transferred to a shelter upstate where she was held in protective custody. Sadly, that shelter planned to euthanize her once the trial was over, rather than evaluate Monkey as an individual. AFF had Monkey brought to them, so she could have a fair shot at the second chance she deserved. Monkey Business is currently up for adoption and living in a foster home where her foster "mom" helps her keep a diary of her daily activities. She is appropriately named because she loves to monkey around. Her smile is contagious, as is her willingness to embrace whatever fun comes her way—a game of tug, a snuggle or even a "zoomies" lap or two around the yard, and she is happy. She is a lovely lady who charms every person she meets, even making friends with the older ladies in her neighborhood, who come by the yard to pet her whenever she is outside. People often cross the street to meet the friendly dog who is wagging her tail so enthusiastically. Monkey has a few dog friends she enjoys, but her true love is her foster "mom." They do everything together. Monkey Business has shown the world that dogs seized from fighting operations deserve to be evaluated as individuals and that when given the opportunity, dogs like Monkey can go on to shine.

TANKGIRL

PENNSYLVANIA
TANKGIRL'S FAVORITE THINGS: THE FOUR CATS SHE LIVES WITH & JUMPING ON THE TRAMPOLINE
ADOPTED FROM ANIMAL FRIENDS

A boy was dragging an 8-week-old puppy who could not walk well down the street; she was suffering from malnutrition from being taken from her mother too soon. A man rescued her from the young boy and brought her in to Animal Friends, where Samantha Ginsburg was a volunteer. For Samantha, it was love at first sight. After two weeks, the man did not come back, and Samantha was then allowed to adopt her. Today, Tankgirl loves to hang out with Samantha & husband, Stephen Streibig. Sweet Tankgirl loves people, snuggling and giving kisses. People often stop to say how beautiful she is, and then Tankgirl tries to crawl in their laps and lick their faces. Tankgirl has come with a price tag though. They call her "the $10,000 dog." She has had every health issue you could imagine: yeast infections, incontinence, bacterial skin infections, allergies (she gets allergy shots every 10 days), root canals mast cell tumors... Tankgirl, though, is the one who hit the jackpot. Not only did she find a home willing to take the time to sort out her many allergies (thankfully, all of her health issues are now under control), but she also found a home willing to deal with her major separation issues and noise anxiety, which have caused her to destroy everything from mattresses and walls to doors, cars and furniture. Samantha said, "She found me for a reason...She gets the best of everything." It has all been worth it to them, for all that Tankgirl gives them in return. As Samantha said, "She is full of pure love."

82

BROOKLYN

NEW YORK
A WONDERFULLY SWEET, HAPPY-GO-LUCKY GIRL WHO WANTS TO PLAY ALL THE TIME
AKA BROOKIE BROOK & LIL' LADY
ADOPTED FROM A CO-WORKER

Brooklyn had been given as a gift to someone who did not want a dog. As a result, Brooklyn was shuffled around from place to place for the first five months of her life. Lesson to be learned: No animals should ever be given to anyone as a surprise. Brooklyn wound up with a co-worker of Jennifer Danino. When the co-worker was no longer able to keep her, Jen took her in. Brooklyn loves all people. She trots up to every human, dog and child with her tail spinning like a helicopter rotor and a huge grin on her face. She also loves all dogs—big, small, male or female, it does not matter. Jen recently started fostering a male pit bull from animal control who was rescued on the day he was scheduled to be put down. He & Brooklyn have become fast friends. While Brooklyn enjoys running after the pigeons, playing fetch, and eating vanilla ice cream, belly rubs and baths are her all-time favorite activities. Jen has never seen a dog enjoy a bath more. Oftentimes, Jen will come home to find paw prints and toys in the bathtub. Brooklyn is spoiled rotten, gets long walks, goes swimming in a nearby lake and visits off-leash dog parks. Now that Brooklyn is in her forever home, she is the "Queen of the Castle." Jen has moved once since she got Brooklyn, and Brooklyn was fine with the move; Jen remained the one constant for Brooklyn, and Brooklyn knows Jen will always be there for her.

84

Martha was walking in town with Vixen one night, when she was surrounded by a group of children. The one adult who was with them stood off to the side watching and smiling. The oldest girl, who was maybe 15, asked, "Is that one of those killer dogs?" Meanwhile, a few of the younger children were getting kisses from Vixen. Martha replied, "No, she is a pit bull. Does she look like a killer?" The girl agreed she did not and was soon right down with the rest of them. The mom said, "I guess they really do get a bad rap, don't they?"

VIXEN

NEW MEXICO

VERY HIGH ENERGY, SO LESSONS, DOGGY DAY CARE, THE DOG PARK & AGILITY ARE ALL NEEDED

AKA LITTLE GIRL & TROUBLE

FOSTERED THROUGH WATERMELON MOUNTAIN RANCH (WMR) & GENTLE SOULS SANCTUARY (GSS)

Vixen lived from puppyhood with a single mom and her two children. No one had time for her. She was in the yard alone all day. She started jumping over the fence and running down the street to find friends. Her family then tied her up in the yard. When she was 6 months old, she contracted parvo and survived. A neighbor felt sorry for her and convinced the "owner" to spay Vixen and hand her over to a rescue. WMR was full, so the neighbor contacted GSS, who then contacted Martha Kennedy about fostering her. A few days later, Martha picked her up in Albuquerque with Ziggy (see pgs. 88 & 89). Their meeting in a casino parking lot went well, and so did her meeting at home with Martha's female elderbull, Bomber. Vixen was underweight and had a dull coat, so good food and exposure/socialization were in order, too. Martha had always wanted a pocket pittie, and after seeing that Vixen & Ziggy were becoming best friends, Martha was ready to keep her. Vixen has now earned her Canine Good Citizen certificate and is learning agility. Vixen is "The Great Hunter." Lizards and rabbits are her specialty. She keeps herself entertained for hours in the backyard looking out for lizards. She is also "The Great Tormenter"...of Ziggy, at least. For example, she likes to leap at him, and then spin in the air and hit him with her backside. To Martha, Vixen is her hiking partner, companion at her art show openings and traveling buddy—she's a wonderful little friend to share life's joys with.

ZIGGY

NEW MEXICO
ZIGGY EARNED HIS CANINE GOOD CITIZEN CERTIFICATE & IS LEARNING AGILITY
ADOPTED FROM COLORADO PIT BULL RESCUE (CPBR)

Ziggy was just a 3-month-old puppy when he was picked up in Denver, which has BSL. Fortunately, he was brought to a shelter outside the city, so his life was spared. He was there until 9 months of age when he started to shut down and stopped eating. CPBR took him in then. He spent the rest of the time with the rescue until Martha Kennedy adopted him, which was not until he was 2.5 years old. Martha was looking on Petfinder.com for an older brindle male pit bull, a little on the small size, when she found Ziggy, a 75-lb. tan boy! Martha & Bomber, Martha's older pit bull, drove 6.5 hours to meet him. Martha fell for him right away—there was such an eagerness to please. He was extremely anxious in this new home, but eventually settled down. He was the first older rescue Martha had adopted and is the one responsible for getting her into learning more about dog behavior, training, agility and rescue. He also inspired Martha to volunteer at the local shelter, especially working with the more difficult dogs—the long-timers. Martha even fostered a few young dogs, but had to stop when she "failed" with the last one, Vixen (see pgs. 86 & 87). Ziggy was a great foster "brother," playing well with the dogs even though they were about half his size. When he is not chasing lizards, he loves to run as fast as he can with Vixen chasing at his heels, and then they roll and wrestle. Ziggy likes to sniff. (It is almost an art form for him. He may start learning nose work soon.) He lifts his head, smells the air and wanders off toward the scent, with a look of spacey bliss on his face.

88

HOOCH

TEXAS
EXPRESSES HIS LOVE BY GIVING THOUSANDS OF KISSES
ADOPTED FROM A FRIEND

Hooch was one of a litter of five puppies. His mother was a very young mother—not even a year old at the time. The mother was slowly rejecting the puppies by the time they were 5 weeks old. That was when Brooke Sipek's friend decided to give them away. Brooke took Hooch and has raised him since that time. Hooch is living the good life now with Brooke & her husband, Brian. American Sign Language (ASL) is used in the home, so Hooch knows both verbal commands and visual ASL commands, too. Hooch is great with other dogs, especially their foster dogs, for whom he is an excellent role model. He loves people so much he would prefer to play with people over dogs. He is also good with kids. Hooch means the whole world to Brooke—they are an inseparable duo. He is a seasoned traveler; having traveled across the U.S. four times, he loves seeing new places. They are in Austin now, where they have settled in with their two other dogs, Chief & Lo. Hooch gets along with them beautifully. Family and friends are amazed to see how affectionate this pit bull is. They can see what a loyal companion he is, and their nephews love to play with Hooch, too. Every morning, Hooch starts his day by crawling under their blankets and snuggling with them for a while. They all enjoy going to dog parks and going on long walks through the woods. Hooch loves to swim, and enjoys doggy ice cream, which he gets on every birthday and sometimes during hot summers.

91

CHOPPERS

TEXAS
CHOPPERS LOVES HIS STUFFED TOYS, PLAYING FETCH & RUNNING TRAILS IN THE WOODS WITH LORI
AKA POPPI & CHOPS
ADOPTED FROM RECYCLED CANINES DALMATIAN RESCUE (RCDR)

Choppers had been picked up as a stray in Montgomery County, Texas. He weighed only 83 lbs. and was heartworm positive. He was in a Houston shelter where bullies are not adopted out to the public—only a rescue could save him from euthanasia. RCDR stepped in, and Lori Salazar, who has been a volunteer at RCDR for the last 10 years, fostered Choppers and fell in love with him. He slowly put on weight and survived heartworm treatment. Lori & her husband, AJ, adopted him. He is one mellow dog who loves other dogs and every person he meets, including children. He enjoys lounging by the pool to sun himself, as well as taking car rides and trips to the dog park. He truly loves life. Choppers lives with his Dalmatian brother, Cooper, who is also a rescue from RCDR. Choppers is a great foster brother and role model for the many RCDR fosters that come in and out of the home. They spend their days going in and out of their doggy door to their backyard, lounging poolside and playing. Choppers sleeps (yes, all 120 lbs.) at the foot of their bed, which he allows them to share. People love him. He is a unique-looking boy, with one beautiful blue eye and one brown, which is usually a conversation starter. He is a total ham and loves attention. When a neighbor first saw Choppers, he asked tentatively, "Is he a pit bull?" Now he loves him and is always excited to see him. Choppers is a gentle, loving soul who was saved from the unthinkable, and he definitely knows it.

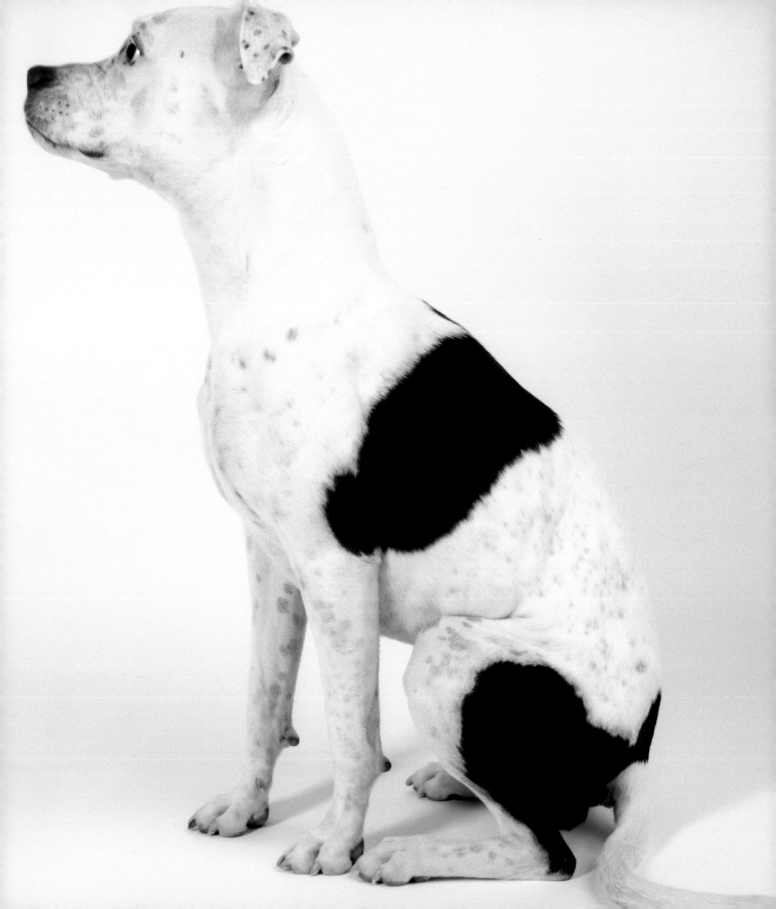

LUNA

NEVADA

FREE-SPIRITED, INDEPENDENT & FUN-LOVING, LUNA LOVES PEOPLE & IS AN ENTHUSIASTIC GREETER
AKA MS. BARK-A-LOT & THE PROPERTY MANAGER
FOUND AS A STRAY

Veronica Selco was taking Macho & Beauty (*see pgs. 100 & 101*) to the dog park one day when she found Luna on a street corner. She was about 9 months of age and very shy. The shelter knew her. Veronica wondered how such a cute and sweet dog could go unclaimed, but she did. And so Veronica & her husband, Scott, kept her. This escape artist quickly showed them how she wound up on the streets in the first place—climbing on tables to jump over walls and opening doors in the house, including the back door! Luna has come far, but is still a little shy at times. Luna is an "ambassadog." She and the other members of what Veronica calls her "Bully Brigade" (*see pg. 51*) have inspired Veronica to get involved in education, advocacy and rescue work for bully breeds in their area, even starting a website: bullyambassadogs.com. Her message to the public: "Dogs are individuals! Punish the deed, not the 'breed!'" Luna has an active Vegas lifestyle—hiking, swimming and romping in the snow. This athletic girl's favorite activities are chasing the lure in sprint racing and sniffing around in nose work. Luna trains for fun and competition in flyball, nose work and weight pulling, and she has held titles in DockDogs and sprint racing. Luna is one of the fastest racing pit bulls in the All Breed Lure Sports Association, and so Veronica is starting an affiliate club in town for her.

ZOEY

GEORGIA

ZOEY LOVES TO CUDDLE WITH HER BFF, A 12-YEAR-OLD BLACK-&-WHITE CAT WHO LOOKS LIKE HER
ADOPTED FROM A FRIEND

Thanksgiving week 2010, Zoey was rescued off the streets of Atlanta by one of Laura Mudrow's friends. Having been a stray for some time, she was severely underweight, with hip bones and ribs protruding, and was covered in mange, which had caused sores, bumps and hair loss. She smelled horrible and was lethargic and scared. Their friends started to nurse her back to health. As soon as Laura saw her pictures, she was drawn to this beautiful dog. She & her husband, Gary, went to visit her and saw that despite her sad past, her personality was huge. By the time they adopted her, she had gained weight, but had lost most of her fur. She still has a few bare spots. As she gained strength, her energy level increased, and her puppy playfulness emerged. Now 2 years old—she rules the house, or at least tries to. She greets Laura & Gary for at least five minutes when they come home. Zoey lives with "brother" Vishnu (*see pgs. 98 & 99*) and four cats. When Vishnu has his leash on, Zoey parades him around the house with his leash in her mouth. They discovered her love of water (she even loves puddles) after a worker at Zoey's day care told Laura how difficult it was to get Zoey out of the kiddie pool that day. That weekend, they took her to the lake, for the first time, where she quickly did a swan dive into the water. She zooms around the house (with brief stops to look out the window) and uses both couches as part of her racetrack. She has no problem entertaining herself.

VISHNU

GEORGIA
VISHNU HAS GREAT FACIAL EXPRESSIONS & FOCUS; HE DRAWS PEOPLE TO HIM IN ANY SITUATION
ADOPTED FROM BEST FRIENDS ANIMAL SOCIETY (BFAS)

Eight-month-old Vishnu was found wandering the streets of New Orleans about six weeks after Hurricane Katrina. He had experienced recent trauma that resulted in total blindness in his right eye. Vishnu was rescued by BFAS and sent to a foster group, but after the place was shut down, Vishnu was sent to BFAS. He was chosen to be the run mate of Meryl, one of the most reactive Vicktory dogs, because he was so easygoing. He had been at BFAS for a couple years when Laura Mudrow & her husband, Gary, volunteered at the sanctuary. The staff suggested they take Vishnu (formerly known as "Fisher") as their sleepover dog. After hearing his story, they agreed to take him for the night. They were not looking to adopt another dog, but after spending some time with him and experiencing his huge heart, they decided to adopt him. BFAS took them through the adoption process, and within two months, Vishnu was on a plane to Atlanta. During those two months, one of their other dogs was diagnosed with cancer and passed away three weeks after Vishnu arrived. Vishnu's importance to the family was obvious, as he helped them through a hard time. He now lives with their other dog, Zoey (see pgs. 96 & 97), and four cats. The blindness in his one eye does not hold him back. Vishnu has the potential to be damaged due to his past, but he is very well-adjusted and trusting. He is the happiest dog ever. Laura & Gary are so grateful their paths crossed with his.

MACHO

NEVADA
SWEET NATURED & HANDSOME
AKA MACHO LIBRE
ADOPTED FROM A CO-WORKER

A co-worker of Scott Selco made the mistake of not fixing her dogs, who then produced an "accidental" litter. Scott & his wife, Veronica, rescued their two pups, Macho & Beauty (see pg. 101), just in time before parvo struck and killed the litter. They were just 4 months old. At the time, Scott & Veronica were renovating their home, and so the dogs are very well-socialized due to their exposure to many people and noises at a young age. Macho is the only male dog in what Veronica calls her "Bully Brigade" (see pgs. 51, 94 & 95) and her "ambassadogs," who have inspired Veronica to get involved in education, advocacy and rescue work for bully breeds in their community. Macho's best friend is his sister Beauty. Macho has earned his Canine Good Citizen certificate and is a registered therapy dog. He trains for fun and competition in flyball, nose work, DockDogs, sprint racing, weight pulling and doggy drill team. When they first started visiting nursing homes for therapy work, Macho & Beauty were both turned down at a facility because of their "breed," but they did not let that stop them. Macho loves people and "has never met a stranger." Veronica said, "He's the kind of dog that looks in your eyes and comforts your soul!" Macho & Veronica spend a lot of time in the public eye, where they are happy to show people what pit bulls are really like.

BEAUTY

NEVADA
FRIENDLY & PUPPYLIKE, BEAUTY LOVES TO LOOK OUT THE WINDOW FOR THE NEIGHBOR'S CATS
AKA MISS NEVADA
ADOPTED FROM A CO-WORKER

A co-worker of Scott Selco made the mistake of not fixing her dogs, who then produced an "accidental" litter. Scott & his wife Veronica rescued their two pups, Beauty & Macho (see pg. 100), just in time before parvo struck and killed the litter. They were just 4 months old. Beauty, at the age of 9 months, was diagnosed with a exocrine pancreatic insufficiency (EPI), a serious medical condition. EPI is difficult to diagnose and even when diagnosed some dogs are not responsive to medication. Because the medication is expensive, and because the treatment is ongoing, some families choose to euthanize dogs that are diagnosed with EPI. Fortunately, Beauty responded well to the medication and is thriving despite her disease. Beauty is the oldest female at "Casa Los Pits" (see pgs. 51, 94 & 95). Beauty's best friend is her brother, Macho. Beauty has earned her Canine Good Citizen certificate and is a registered therapy dog. People love her for her beauty and her friendliness. She loves to fetch squeaky balls, play in the snow, swim and run errands with Veronica. Beauty is a fast racer, and loves flyball, nose work and DockDogs, although she is taking a break from strenuous activities now due to a knee injury.

SYDNEY

CALIFORNIA
ALWAYS HAPPY SYDNEY—IF YOU SAY HER NAME TO HER WHILE SHE IS NAPPING, HER TAIL WILL WAG
AKA SYDSYDS, SISI & SISI MAGOO
ADOPTED FROM BAD RAP

Sydney is a special dog with a special history. Donna Reynolds & Tim Racer of BAD RAP were in New Orleans after Hurricane Katrina to help the many dogs, in particular the pit bulls, that were lost and homeless after the storm. Donna once said that Sydney was their "no brainer" rescue because she was so warm and friendly. Sydney lived in New Orleans, where she had been a mother to many, many puppies. Hurricane Katrina left her stranded on a rooftop, where she waited for help for two weeks. She was one of 10 dogs that Donna & Tim flew back to California to start a new life. Sydney was chosen out of the 10 to go to a shelter that did not usually adopt out pit bulls. The shelter made an exception for one Katrina dog. Why Sydney? Because she had such a great temperament and had a job to do—to prove how lovely and adoptable pit bulls really are. That all changed when they found out Sydney was heartworm positive. She had to stay in foster care for eight months to recover. That is when Katie Moyer first saw her online and fell in love with "Princess Sydney." Sydney was also how Katie first found BAD RAP, where she now volunteers. Sydney is a great role model and big "sister" to the many foster pit bulls who come into their home. Sydney lives life to the fullest and never looks back. She has earned her Canine Good Citizen certificate. She loves people, naps in the sun, fly chasing and her "brother," Toby (see pgs. 104 & 105).

TOBY

CALIFORNIA
TOBY IS VERY PATIENT WITH THE MANY FOSTER DOGS HE HAS WELCOMED INTO HIS HOME
AKA TOBERS, TOBIAS, TOBLERONE & TOBETOBES
ADOPTED FROM SANTA CRUZ COUNTY ANIMAL SERVICES (SCCAS)

A child witnessed Toby being thrown from a moving car. The child's mother took pity on Toby and took him to SCCAS, which fixed him up and made him available for adoption. Katie Moyer found him by chance. She was wandering though the shelter one day when she was 19 years old and saw him. She reached out her hand to him, even though she was slightly scared of pit bulls back then, and he wagged his tail, doing a "wiggle butt." Katie was hooked and adopted him. Since adopting Toby, Katie has fostered pit bulls through BAD RAP and has hosted countless different rescue pit bulls. In addition, Katie has volunteered at three different shelters, always looking out for pit bulls. She is also active in spay/neuter outreach and political activism for the "breed." Toby is the root of her inspiration. Toby & his "sister" Sydney (see pgs. 102 & 103) are like an old married couple. They do everything together. They each get a little anxious when the other is away. Toby has earned his Canine Good Citizen certificate, and he is a certified therapy dog. He is a champ with the elderly and has visited retirement homes in the past. He greets all strangers with a smile and a tail wag. He loves his outings and slow walks, where he stops and smells the flowers and encourages Katie to do the same. He also hogs the bed every night. Katie said, "I took him home knowing nothing about dogs. I got really lucky. He is gentle, kind and sensitive. He is my joy."

LUCY

CALIFORNIA
SWEET, LOVING, LOYAL GIRL IN NEED OF A FOREVER HOME
UP FOR ADOPTION AT KARMA RESCUE

Beautiful Lucy was found roaming the streets of Los Angeles pregnant and abandoned. A nice family rescued her, but they already had a number of dogs and could not afford to keep her. Shortly after they took her in, she gave birth to a litter of puppies. In early 2011, the family relinquished her. She may have been in a home before since she already has good manners and walks well on leash. She is a young, gentle and playful girl who likes people, kids and other dogs. When this book went to print, Karma Rescue had helped place all but one of her pups, and Lucy was still looking for a forever home of her own.

TACOMA

UTAH

LOVES OTHER ANIMALS; HE HAS TRIED TO PLAY WITH CHICKENS, BABY CALVES, GOATS & SHEEP
ADOPTED FROM BEST FRIENDS ANIMAL SOCIETY (BFAS)

Animal control in Kanab, UT, picked up Tacoma, who was found running loose with another dog. BFAS took the dogs in, but Tacoma did not do well in the kennel. He chewed and chewed on his tail to the point where it had to be amputated. BFAS tried everything to relieve his anxiety. When Traci Madson contacted BFAS to inquire about adopting one of the Vicktory dogs, they told her that none were available yet but asked whether she might be interested in Tacoma. The sanctuary allows visitors to take pets overnight for a sleepover, and that is what Traci did with Tacoma. He slept right by her all night, and she knew he was hers for good. Traci decided to get him certified as a therapy dog after she got him home and saw how he welcomed visitors to the house by climbing up on the couch and resting his head on their laps. Once certified, people were initially hesitant around him due to his "breed," but after they spent time with him, they fell in love with him. Now he visits an assisted living center and will lie next to the residents while they pet him. He also participates in the "I Read to Animals" program, where he goes into a library and has children read to him. One day, after the kids were finished reading to him, one of the mothers approached Traci and said, "He makes me want to go out and get a pit bull. I had no idea they could be so sweet." Tacoma also has earned his Canine Good Citizen certificate and is currently working toward getting certified as a service dog.

107

MIA

WASHINGTON
SHE GIVES PEOPLE HUGS JUST SO SHE CAN SCAN THE COUNTER FOR FOOD
AKA MEEMSY
ADOPTED FROM SEATTLE ANIMAL SHELTER (SAS)

Mia was impounded by the police when she was just 6 weeks old after her owner was arrested for drugs. She was kept in the cat room at SAS since she was too small to be in the dog kennel. Arlene Larsson was volunteering at the shelter and was asked to foster her. She declined, but at the end of the day, workers put Mia in a crate and asked Arlene to "give it a try." She brought Mia home and fell in love. That was 10 years ago. Since then, Mia has been her constant companion through thick and thin. They have hiked, biked with the K-9 cruiser, run on the beach and gone to training and agility classes. Mia got Arlene interested in working with breed rescue, and Arlene has now fostered over a dozen pit bulls. Mia loves people, and people love her. She goes to work with Arlene at SAS to be a "breed" ambassador and to work the crowd for treats. Arlene said, "Mia has changed so many people's minds about pit bulls! She changed my life forever for the better!" Today, Mia lives with Arlene & her husband, Karl, a cat named Rocket, who is her nap buddy, and pit bull "brother," Rupert. She likes to tease Rupert by digging a hole in the yard and then guarding it so he cannot get to it. She also enjoys collar shopping and visiting her "grandparents." "Grandpa" is a big contributor to any of Mia's weight issues over the years. However, Mia is very good at pouting for her benefit...and "her benefit" always involves food.

NALA

CALIFORNIA
UP FOR ADOPTION AT KARMA RESCUE

Three-year-old Nala was rescued from a hoarding situation in the Mojave Desert. Nala makes everyone smile, is eager to please and is a fast learner. She is good with kids. Energetic Nala enjoys long walks and hikes, playing with dogs and cuddling. She would make a great running partner.

MILES

CALIFORNIA
UP FOR ADOPTION AT KARMA RESCUE

Two-year-old Miles has a zest for life. He was relinquished by a family that did not want him any longer. Professionally trained and a fast learner, this smart boy has a fun, goofy side, too. A champion cuddler, Miles is very sweet and likes kids and other dogs. He has great house manners, is good on leash and loves, loves, loves going on walks and giving kisses.

ANGEL BABY

COLORADO
SHE NOW KNOWS LOVE & NEVER HAS TO BE HUNGRY OR LIVE IN FEAR OF BEING HURT AGAIN
ADOPTED FROM PEANUT'S PLACE BULLY RESCUE (PPBR)

One night, Angel Baby was duct-taped inside a box and dumped at a high-kill Texas shelter. Two days later, she gave birth to 12 pups—eight died. She was skin and bones and had dark circles under her eyes and a large gash across her nose, likely from a 2x4. Renee, who runs PPBR in Colorado, found her online just days before she and her pups were due to be euthanized. Renee got them pulled from the shelter and transported to PPBR. A year later, Sherry Moore and a friend got word from Best Friends Animal Society of a rescue that needed help. They then went into action, brought a crew in to help build better shelter for the dogs and recruited volunteers to help on a regular basis. Out of the 52 dogs there, Sherry came upon Angel Baby, who could not use one of her back legs. Sherry got her operated on for a popped patella. She was just going to foster her, but wound up falling for her. Angel Baby slowly got over her fear of almost everything. She is still shy at times with new people and dogs, but she warms up quickly. Angel Baby's life today is idyllic. She lives in the countryside on 10 fenced-in acres with Sherry's two other dogs. On summer nights, Sherry and the dogs sit outside by the fire while Sherry roasts them hot dogs. BSL is rampant in nearby areas, but not in Sherry's area, which is why she chose to live there. People who know Angel Baby adore her; those who do not are often afraid, but Sherry & Angel Baby try to "win them over to the sunny side of the street." Angel Baby lives up to her name 100 percent of the time. She has a big, happy personality and a wiggly butt to go with it.

112

CENTJE
CALIFORNIA
"CENTJE" MEANS "LITTLE COIN" IN DUTCH
ADOPTED FROM SMILEY DOG RESCUE (SDR)

Centje and his three littermates were surrendered to a shelter in Fresno or the East Bay when they were approximately 9 weeks old. SDR took them in and fostered all four puppies before putting them up for adoption. Jackie Shen adopted Centje in late December 2009, and he has been with her ever since. She keeps in touch with the couple who adopted his brother, and they try to meet for playdates every so often. Centje is very athletic and playful, and he loves his toys. He also likes to cuddle, go for walks, play at the dog park and sunbathe. He is extremely food-motivated, which made him very easy to train. Centje is the only dog in the household, but Jackie would like to adopt another puppy, after Centje gets a little older. He goes to doggy day care once or twice a week, which he loves. Jackie believes this is one of the reasons he is so well-socialized. On the other days, he is out with his dog walker and their playgroup. Weekends are when Jackie gets to spend quality time with her puppy. They enjoy life around the Bay Area, going to one of the many dog parks or meeting up with friends and their dogs for a more exciting outing. Point Isabel is a favorite.

HENDRIX

WISCONSIN
JESSICA'S MOTHER CALLS HENDRIX HER "GRANDPIBBLE"
AKA DRIXY
FOSTERED & THEN ADOPTED

Hendrix spent his early days tied up outside, skinny and shivering from the cold. His owner was in jail, and so the man's father was watching him. A woman wound up paying $60 to the man for Hendrix, after she learned he was not feeding the dog and had put him in a storage locker, all because he went to the bathroom inside. The woman could not keep Hendrix, though, since her dog was dog aggressive. Hendrix was taken in by others until Jessica Burch fostered him when he was 3 months old. She was only going to keep him until a forever home was found, but she could not give him up. When she adopted him, Hendrix was emaciated. She got him eating but was soon worried because he was not learning his name. After some testing, including clanking steel bowls by his head while he slept, she discovered he was deaf. Once she started training him using hand signals, he caught on quickly, making great eye contact and looking to Jessica for commands and praise. He has a great life now. Hendrix loves to be outside, no matter what the weather is like. In the summertime, he loves to play in his kiddie pool. In the wintertime, he loves to paw at the snow until he breaks off a piece of ice, which he will hit around like a hockey puck. Hendrix gets along with all dogs. He loves to visit his "grandparents" and play with his canine "aunt" and "uncle"—two Akitas. He is beyond spoiled! He has been such a joy for Jessica's whole family, who love him beyond words.

116

MARTHA

PENNSYLVANIA
MARTHA LOOKS LIKE "A FOOTBALL WITH FOUR LEGS"
ADOPTED FROM ANIMAL RESCUE LEAGUE OF WESTERN PA

Animal control found Martha loose on the streets and called her owner. He took her back. She was later found eating out of a McDonald's dumpster (as Dora said, it was "probably the happiest day of her life"). The owner was called, and he decided he did not want her back. And so, back to the shelter she went. Paul & Dora Magovern were looking for a dog to keep their other dog Bruno (*see pgs. 120 & 121*) company, due to his bad separation anxiety. Martha got Paul with her big, soulful eyes, and won Dora over by running onto her lap and licking her face. Her favorite thing to do is lie on top of Paul & Dora with her head on her paws, staring directly up at them. She loves going for runs with them; she gets into a zone—just trots along, throws her ears back and keeps on trucking. Bruno & Martha live the good life. They live in harmony with Cavalier King Charles Spaniel, Kelly, and cat, Dolly. Martha runs the show, but she lets Kelly think that he is the boss. When he was a puppy and Dolly a kitten, Martha would sit and watch them eat her food. Some people do look nervous when they see Bruno & Martha, but then they see the little Cavalier trotting alongside and realize that they must be harmless. The dogs love nothing more than to snuggle. Paul & Dora have a sense that their dogs are so grateful. They are their first pit bulls. Dora said, "I am 200,000 percent dedicated to the 'breed' now. Moreover, I am constantly amazed at their ability to love and forgive." Dora now volunteers for a pit bull advocacy group (Hello Bully) and plans on only adopting pits in the future.

BRUNO

PENNSYLVANIA
PEOPLE STOP THEM ON THE STREET TO COMMENT ON HOW STRIKINGLY HANDSOME BRUNO IS
AKA B & B-MAN
ADOPTED FROM ANIMAL RESCUE LEAGUE OF WESTERN PA

Bruno was in at least one other home and was returned to the shelter before Paul Magovern adopted him. He is extremely sweet but has been destructive in the past. He has destroyed the interior of a car, countless down comforters, hats, bags, garbage cans and coats—you name it, he has destroyed it. However, he is much calmer now that he has his two canine companions. He now lives with Paul & his wife, Dora, Martha (*see pgs. 118 & 119*) and Kelly, a Cavalier King Charles Spaniel, who is his BFF. Bruno & Kelly are attached at the hip—so much so that they now share a crate. Every night, Martha & Bruno get big rawhides. Kelly follows Bruno and eats the chips that Bruno flakes off. Eventually, Bruno gets thirsty and walks off to get a drink, and then Kelly steals his rawhide stub. Bruno is such a gentle dog that despite weighing 55 lbs. more than Kelly, he will just sit there and bark in protest. He never manages to steal the bone back unless his "parents" intervene for him. He knows his size and plays appropriately with small dogs. He lies down and lets Kelly attack him. When he is excited, say when someone comes to the door, he gets a toy, brings it to the person and wags his entire body and tail. Paul was losing his father when he adopted Bruno, and Bruno served as a source of sanity, comfort and support for Paul. Bruno is truly a 70-lb. lapdog with a heart of gold.

GOZER

RHODE ISLAND
GREAT WITH KIDS
AKA THE GOZ, GOZER THE GOZERIAN, GOZER THE DESTROYER & GOZER THE TRAVELER
ADOPTED FROM HANDSOME DAN'S RESCUE (HDR)

For unknown reasons, Gozer was surrendered by his original owners to Providence Animal Rescue League. The rescue then asked HDR to take him and help modify some of his less desirable behaviors. Several months after his last pit bull passed away, Patrick King was looking for a dog on Petfinder.com and found Gozer. He drove to meet him and his foster "mother," the founder of HDR, Heather Gutshall (see pg. 146). A week later, he adopted Gozer, and they have been together ever since. They met with a large informal dog group during the week and on weekends, they would go hiking, camping or on road trips. A year later, Patrick was looking at apartments near Heather's and dropped by her house with Gozer to say, "Hi!" After mentioning why he was in town, Heather pointed out an available apartment right across the street from her house. He moved in, and Gozer joined her Outbound Hounds Pack on day trips during the week. During that time, Patrick's girlfriend, Deanna Casanovas, adopted Betsy (see pg. 49) from HDR. Gozer loves to wrestle with his "sister." They frequently exchange bones they are chewing on. He is great with people and amazing with children. As much as people cross the street to avoid this pit bull, there are others who cross the street to pet him and comment on how handsome he is (he likes those people better).

JELLY BEAN

A victim of cruelty, Jelly Bean was held as part of the Court Case Dog Program through Safe Humane Chicago. Two-year-old Jelly Bean then came to AFF, where she is now available for adoption. She loves her foster home that she shares with her foster "brother" pit bull, Patrick. Despite her sad start in life, this little "blue" girl does not let that get her down. Her foster "mom" says Jelly Bean is "the most carefree, happy-go-lucky dog" she has ever met. "She loves life!" Sweet and petite, people are naturally drawn to her. She is great with people and a "rock star" with children. She wins over everyone she meets, including many members of her local community. Some neighbors were afraid of Patrick, but after seeing Patrick with little Jelly Bean, they now are unafraid of approaching and petting both dogs. At a recent community day celebration, she marched in a parade and gained fans thanks to her infectious, exuberant personality...and her pink-and-orange tutu! She was so cute she was even featured in a local newspaper article about the event. Jelly Bean's enthusiasm for life shows up in everything she does, from her penchant for kissing everyone she meets, to the way she likes to "help out" with daily activities that go on at home, especially assisting with the dishes. Jelly Bean is a special dog who is determined to have fun, no matter what.

MARTHA WASHINGTON

NEW YORK
MARTHA WORE A STRING OF PEARLS TO MEET THE PRESIDENT OF HSUS AT A BLACK-TIE GALA
AKA THE DONKEY
ADOPTED FROM PHILADELPHIA ANIMAL CARE & CONTROL

Martha lived with a very nice woman who raised her for eight years. When the woman fell on hard times and lost her house, she made the difficult decision to surrender Martha to a shelter. Kim Wolf & Thad Stringer adopted Martha, and through Facebook, they were able to track down her previous owner, who shared stories and photos of Martha. Martha was a well-trained, socialized and balanced dog who fit right into their household. She shares her home with two other former First Ladies, Mary Todd Lincoln (a Pug) and Nancy Reagan (a Cocker Spaniel). Martha loves to dispel myths. Some say two pit bulls cannot live together—she has now lived with three (*see pgs. 130 & 131*). Some say old dogs cannot learn new tricks—she became a certified therapy dog at 9.5 years old! (Kim & Thad are working on getting her ears to touch on command, but now she just does that when something interests her.) Everyone loves Martha, and Martha loves everyone. Kim & Thad bring her everywhere because nothing fazes her. She often goes to work with Kim at Animal Farm Foundation. This social butterfly is proving elderbulls are not ready for the retirement home just yet. Martha brings youthful energy and enthusiasm to everything she does. Her favorite activities are swimming, going to happy hour/out to dinner, attending galas, marching in parades and visiting libraries to let children practice their reading skills by reading to her. Life is a party to Martha, and, in Martha's mind, she *is* the party.

124

PIGGLY WIGGLY

NEW YORK
PIG GOT HIS NAME FROM HIS WIGGLING REAR & HIS PIGLIKE NOSE
AKA PIG & THE PIG
FOUND AS A STRAY

Kathleen Pierce found a stray 5-month-old pit bull wandering the streets of downtown Albany. She had just lost her beloved dog, Hermie, and was in no place to be thinking about adopting another dog. She soon found Pig's owner, but he wanted nothing to do with this overly friendly, wiggling, adorable puppy. By then, this sweetheart of a dog had won Kathleen over, and Pig had found his forever home. Pig came to live with her other dogs and a few cats. Kathleen adopted former Michael Vick dog Jhumpa Jones (see pgs. 152 & 153) several years later, and he could not have been more thrilled with his new "sister." He helped show her the ropes and taught her how to live in a home environment. He has helped change attitudes about pit bull type dogs through his therapy work and his work as a humane educator in dozens of classrooms across New York state, at numerous events, and through his Facebook page called "I Dig the Pig." He is also involved in Paws-to-Read programs in the capital district of New York. Pig is a certified therapy dog, a reading assistance dog to children and is ATTS temperament tested. He was the first-ever pit bull therapy dog at Albany Medical Center. He is Kathleen's love and joy.

125

MCCOY

NEW YORK
A CHAMPION GOOFBALL & SWIMMER
AKA THE REAL MCCOY
UP FOR ADOPTION AT ANIMAL FARM FOUNDATION (AFF)

Because his owners let him roam off leash, McCoy took every opportunity he could to "cruise" around the city and make new friends. Needless to say, McCoy became "a regular" at his local Iowa City animal shelter. At last, his owners decided they were not responsible enough, and so they surrendered him to the shelter for good. McCoy was then transferred to AFF, where he is now available for adoption. Two-year-old McCoy is smart, affectionate and good-natured and lives life with gusto. A mix of rugged good looks and goofiness, this handsome boy often has a bubble of slobber hanging out of his mouth. He is a true adventurer—loving to play with other dogs, to meet new people and to try new things. He changes minds and opens hearts everywhere he goes...and he goes a lot of places, including frequent "vacations" to his foster home in the Big Apple. However, this athletic boy's all-time favorite activity is swimming. McCoy is great with children, too. He volunteers at the library for their "Read to the Dogs" program, where elementary school kids practice their reading skills by reading to their canine friends. One time a first grader was so tickled that she and McCoy had the same color hair, that she got over her fear of reading aloud and giggled throughout the entire visit.

Canine Disc (retired)
2007 Purina Incredible Dog Challenge National Champion
2006 Cynosport World Champion
Multiple-time Skyhoundz World Finalist
Multiple-time UFO World Finalist
Multiple-time AWI World Finalist

Weight Pulling (retired)
WP-2 Weight Pulling
(pulled more than 30 times his body weight)
WP-CH Weight Pull Champion

WALLACE

MINNESOTA
HIS MOTTO: "CHANGING MINDS, ONE DISC AT A TIME"
AKA THE PIT BULL
ADOPTED FROM NORTHCENTRAL WORKING DOG CLUB (NWDC)

Rehomed as a puppy after his owner died, Wallace was then surrendered to the shelter when he was 2 years old. This smart, high-energy dog deteriorated rapidly in a shelter environment with little to no mental or physical activity. He was in danger of being euthanized. Clara Yori, who worked at the shelter, and her husband, Andrew ("Roo"), knew all Wallace needed was a home and an outlet for his energy. The Yoris finally persuaded the shelter, which viewed this pit bull as a "liability" and would not let Wallace be fostered out, to let them foster him through NWDC. The Yoris soon discovered Wallace had the highest drive of any dog they had ever seen and was a natural at disc. They adopted him. Roo worked with Wallace, entered him in competitions, and the rest is history. Roo & Wallace competed in disc events all over the country. Wallace surpassed any expectations they could have imagined. Wallace got attention, especially as a pit bull succeeding in a sport typically dominated by herding breeds. People loved him! Here was an opportunity to change people's minds about pit bulls. It was not uncommon for people to approach them after an event to say they used to not like pit bulls, but after seeing Wallace perform and meeting him, their minds had changed (it is nearly impossible to hate a cute dog playing disc). Wallace's talents on the field have opened the minds of countless spectators over the years. The Yoris feel fortunate that they have been able to reach people this way. A true inspiration, showing what one can overcome to succeed, Wallace has earned the respect of people from all over the world. He has appeared in countless magazines, as well as on ABC, ESPN2 and Animal Planet. Wallace has many accomplishments (*see pg. 128*)—all this from a former shelter dog that many thought was not worth saving. Wallace has had many health problems, and his latest health issues have benched him. He has lived an action-packed life, but at the age of 9, he is now enjoying a well-deserved retirement, where he dines on the best dog food, and his only title is "champion snuggler." He shares his home with five dogs, including "brother" Hector (*see pgs. 140 & 141*) and his BFF Angus. His story is told in the movie, "Wallace: The Rise of an Underdog" and on his website (wallacethepitbull.com) and his Facebook fan page.

- **2010 Humane Educator of the Year** (awarded by Philadelphia Mayor Michael Nutter)
- **2010 Philadelphia Barking Beauty Pageant Winner**
- **2010 "Humanitarian Awards" from** *The American Dog Magazine*:
  - First Place for "Animal Welfare Blogger" (for elderbulls.blogspot.com)
  - Third Place for "Therapy Dog Who Gives Unconditionally"

SARGE THE ELDERBULL

NEW YORK
SARGE'S LEGACY LIVES ON THROUGH HIS WEBSITE, FACEBOOK PAGE & PSPCA'S SARGE FUND
AKA THE SARGE-STER
ADOPTED FROM PENNSYLVANIA SPCA (PSPCA)

This is the story of how a victim of animal cruelty became a national celebrity, humane educator and cherished family pet. Sarge's life did not truly begin until he was 14. It was then, in September 2008, that Sarge and 30 other dogs were seized in Philadelphia from an alleged dog fighter with prior animal cruelty convictions. Sarge spent five months in protective custody at the PSPCA, where Kim Wolf worked at the time. Although Sarge had been there for months, she had not given him much thought. She knew she could never adopt him since she had no experience with pit bulls or dogs seized from alleged fighting operations, she believed some of the myths and generalizations about pit bulls, and she already lived with four dogs in a small rowhome. However, when a co-worker asked whether she would take him home so he could "live out his life," which was expected to be another month or two, Kim & her husband, Thad Stringer, gave it a try. And like that, against all odds, this 14.5-year-old pit bull and victim of cruelty got the forever home he had always deserved. Still, Kim remembers looking over her shoulder repeatedly when she was alone in the car with Sarge driving him home from the shelter, just to make sure he was not going to attack her. It did not take long for Sarge to teach Kim that those myths and generalizations she believed were just that—myths and generalizations. Sarge's only scars from his past were physical, but he had many issues: unhealed bite wounds, fractured ribs that were never treated, severe arthritis, anemia, just one tooth and deafness. Sarge took pain medication and supplements for his arthritis. His arthritis was so severe that he had to be carried everywhere. Despite all his ailments and his rough past, he was the "easiest, friendliest, most lovable dog" they had ever met. He assimilated quickly into their household, which included six other dogs, and was the most stable and tolerant dog they had ever had. All this from a pit bull and cruelty case? This was one of many lessons Sarge had for Kim, and as it turned out, the rest of the world. Kim created a website (elderbulls.blogspot.com) and Sarge gained a following. She passed on all of the lessons she was learning from Sarge to the rest of the world through the website and through Facebook. Over the next three years, Sarge taught Kim, who in turn taught others, how to be a better advocate for dogs. He coined the word "elderbull," a proper term to honor senior pit bulls, and taught us that one is never too old to contribute to the community (or to get a girlfriend... their Pug, who loved him instantly, spent their first night together cleaning his ears, a labor of love that would become a nightly ritual). He showed the world that pit bulls are just dogs like any others, asked us not to hold a grudge against abusers, and taught us not to be defined by the past but to focus on the present and to celebrate each new day. "Team Sarge" T-shirts were created to help spread the word. The Sarge Fund was started to provide low-cost spaying/neutering and vet care for Philadelphia's pit bull type dogs. He went on to get certified as a therapy dog and comforted people in nursing homes and rehabilitation centers. He visited schools to educate children about animal issues and appeared on television and the Internet, and in newspapers and magazines. His last three years were a whirlwind. Sarge sadly passed away in July 2011, just a few weeks shy of his 17th birthday. He left a legacy. His life touched thousands, whose hearts and minds were opened by him to all that pit bulls, victims of abuse, and rescued, senior and deaf dogs have to offer us...trust, compassion, forgiveness and love.

130

THE VICK DOGS

In 2007, the world learned that NFL star quarterback Michael Vick had been running a dog fighting operation. For almost six years, Vick and his friends had been breeding, training and fighting pit bulls at Bad Newz Kennels on Vick's property. Sheds painted black were found behind Vick's house. One was an infirmary for the dogs wounded in fights. Others had equipment for training and a "rape stand" for breeding. Fights took place in the biggest shed, where police found a blood-stained room, an outline of a pit on the floor and a dog's tooth on the windowsill. Buried in the backyard were the bodies of dogs. At least 12 dogs, ones that did not fight very well, were killed by Vick and his friends. Some were hanged; others were electrocuted. One dog was slammed repeatedly against the ground until it died. When authorities busted Vick, 51 pit bulls were seized from his property.

At that time, it was a common belief that dogs seized from fight busts could not be saved, that they were uncontrollable, violent and untrustworthy. They were referred to as "kennel trash." They were typically held as evidence until their "owners'" trial was over, and then all of them were euthanized. Many called for the same treatment here. The Humane Society of the United States (HSUS) recommended euthanizing them and called them "...some of the most aggressively trained pit bulls in the country." People for the Ethical Treatment of Animals (PETA) also said they should be put down, stating that "these dogs are ticking time bombs." Statements like these were even being made by people who had never met the dogs. However, there was a public outcry to save them.

A court ordered for the dogs to be evaluated. The ASPCA convened a group of experts, including BAD RAP's founders Donna Reynolds & Tim Racer, to evaluate the dogs. The team examined the dogs individually. Some thought they would only be able to save at most 10 percent of the dogs. They ran each dog through a series of tests and were surprised by what they found. Some were so shy they would "pancake"—flatten and not move off the ground, a few were dog aggressive and almost none were aggressive toward people. Instead of saving just five dogs (10 percent) as originally hoped, 47 of the 51 dogs seized were candidates for rescue: 25 were appropriate for foster homes; and 22 for sanctuary, since they needed further rehabilitation and socialization. Only one dog, who had been fought and bred so much that the dog had had enough of people and life, had to be put down.

These dogs had spent deprived lives caged or chained in the woods. After they were confiscated, they were parceled out to six different Virginia animal control facilities, where they were held as evidence. Here their isolation continued. This confinement, with little socialization or stimulation, was hardest on the young dogs—who during a critical point in their development knew little of the world outside of their small kennels. By the time all of these dogs were released from custody, most had spent more than seven months in isolation.

BAD RAP rented an RV and drove 13 of the dogs that were ready for a foster home back to California. Almost all of the 22 dogs that needed further rehabilitation and socialization went to Best Friends Animal Society (BFAS) in Utah, where they came to be called the "Vicktory Dogs." The remaining dogs were dispersed to smaller rescues. The Vick property was bought by animal rights, rescue and advocacy group Dogs Deserve Better, which is turning the kennel into a rehabilitation facility, "Good Newz," for former penned and chained dogs.

It is important to remember that all of these dogs would have been put down if it had not been for the efforts of a few determined individuals who believed in these dogs and stood up for what they knew was right. As Donna Reynolds said, "Vick showed the worst of us, our bloodlust, but this rescue effort showed the best."

It was not just a dog fighting case, but a hoarding case and a neglect case, as well, since Vick had amassed more dogs than he could fight or sell. Jim Gorant, author of The Lost Dogs, which chronicles the case, said, "For the first time in a legal setting, dogs were viewed not as the implements of a harsh and brutal undertaking, but as the victims of it."

The following pages contain portraits and stories of 10 of the Vick dogs. Some of these dogs were suitable for a foster home, and others were sent to sanctuary at BFAS for rehabilitation. Just as people react differently to the experiences that have shaped them, dogs react differently, too. Sweeping generalizations do not apply. While no two of these dogs had the exact same experiences at Bad Newz Kennels or in custody, they are dealing with their past in their own way and coping the best way they know how. What is clear is that these dogs, despite the opinion of many that these dogs should have been put down, are proving every day to us that they deserved a chance: a chance not only to live, but to live in a loving home where they could let their true selves shine. They are proving they are more than capable of making wonderful pets and of giving love.

The Vick case and these dogs have set a precedent. Most dogs seized from dog fighting busts are now individually evaluated in an attempt to save as many of the stable and well-adjusted ones as possible. HSUS now supports individual evaluations of fighting dogs. These dogs are no longer viewed as "bad dogs" but as victims of crimes perpetrated by human hands. Because of their success, the Vick dogs have given all dogs seized from fight busts a chance at life. They have elevated the public's opinion of pit bulls. They have shown us that all dogs should be treated as individuals. They have shown us what it means to forgive, to trust, to be brave and to love. These are some very special dogs.

Further information about the Vick dogs can be found in the book The Lost Dogs by Jim Gorant.

TEDDLES

CALIFORNIA

THIS 72-LB. LAPDOG LOVES CUDDLES, KISSES, BELLY RUBS & EVERYONE HE MEETS

AKA TED, TEDDY, TED-BABY, TEDLITO & T-MAC

ADOPTED FROM BAD RAP

Teddles was the largest pit bull seized from Bad Newz Kennels. It is believed he was not fought: bigger dogs do not do well in the pit; and he showed signs of having spent time elsewhere. For example, he knew how to climb stairs and jumped up on the couch as if he had done it before. He had also been photographed with Vick for a magazine article back in 2001. Teddles was one of the dogs evaluated as ready for a foster home. Cindy Houser was looking for a companion for her rescued pit bull, Izzi, when she viewed Teddles' "available dog" video on BAD RAP's website. She fell in love with the big, goofy, rambunctious boy. Only after she put in an application did she find out that he was a Vick dog. At first, Teddles had some challenges. He was afraid of train whistles, gunshots from the nearby gun range and his shadow. He guarded food at times and did not know how to play with toys. Today, however, he has triumphed over his past. In 2009, he earned his Canine Good Citizen certificate. Everyone who meets him loves him. Friendly Teddles loves being with his family, going on long walks and car rides, running alongside Cindy's bike, playing fetch for food, wrestling with Izzi and playing with toys. Flirt-pole sessions and his beloved naptime on the sofa rank high on his list of favorite activities, too. He is the happy, well-adjusted family pet of Cindy, her husband, Gil Ramirez, and her mother, Karen Anderson. Cindy said, "We feel so blessed to have Ted in our lives!"

JONNY JUSTICE

CALIFORNIA
ONE-THIRD DOG + ONE-THIRD PIG + ONE-THIRD COW = 100 PERCENT HAM
AKA PIG & PIGGY
ADOPTED FROM BAD RAP

Jonny has starred on the cover of *Parade* magazine, was featured in an article on "Amazing Animals" in *U.S. News & World Report*, was talked about at length in Jim Gorant's *The Lost Dogs*, has appeared as a guest on the *Rachael Ray* show, was showcased on the cover of this book and was mentioned in countless other media outlets...isn't it about time Jonny got an agent? With all of the wonderful, positive press on Jonny, it is easy to forget how far this dog has come. One of the Bad Newz dogs, Jonny spent the first 12 months or so of his life chained outside and the following six months in a Virginia shelter, languishing with little to no stimulation. Things changed for the better when he was driven to BAD RAP. It was not until the USDA signed his evidence release paperwork in late 2007 that he was finally free of his past. He never looked back. Jonny even underwent a name change from Jonny Rotten to Jonny Justice, since he got his justice from Vick and could get justice for pit bulls. Jonny was fostered and then adopted by Cris Cohen. After some downtime, the work of acclimating to a home began. Jonny soon learned that life was more than a kennel or a chain. It was wonderful and exciting. He took it all in as fast as he could. Within 18 months of his being confiscated, he passed the ATTS temperament test, earned his Canine Good Citizen certificate, earned a therapy dog certificate and worked as a reading assistant in a children's literacy program. Jonny also pulls a draft cart for exercise and knows over 30 commands. Cris & Jonny resigned from their therapy program (pit bulls were banned by a city agency); however, he & Jonny continue to be in the public eye educating people about pit bulls, about dogs from fight busts and about forgiveness and trust.

UBA

Uba's image was first seen in the *New York Times* next to the headline "Menacing Dogs Await Their Fate." Sweet and loving Uba is about as far from menacing as you can get. One of the dogs evaluated as ready for a foster home, Uba made the cross-country trip in an RV to BAD RAP, where he was fostered by Letti de Little. Letti fell in love with his intelligence and fun personality and adopted him. Uba now has many dog friends and helps his home's many foster dogs, including other victims of dog fighting, acclimate to the real world. Smart and athletic, Uba knows countless commands, has earned his Canine Good Citizen certificate, competes in rally, has qualified to start his first nose work trial and loves to run on his doggy treadmill. Uba does face challenges, though. He was around 6 months old when he was seized and held in isolation for another six months. Since he lacked any exposure to normal activities for the first very formative year of his life, he can be fearful and shut down in new situations. Letti said, "He has come an extremely long way." People often become emotional when they hear his story, but Letti tries to focus on how lucky he is now and the positive impact the Vick dogs have had for all pit bulls and rescued dogs. "Uba has been a part of this change in perceptions alongside his friends Jonny Justice, Hector, Audie, Zippy...and all the others. He has a profound effect on many who meet him. We have been on an amazing journey together."

HECTOR

MINNESOTA
HIS MOTTOS: "MAKING UP FOR LOST TIME" & "THE ONLY THING I FIGHT IS DISCRIMINATION"
AKA HECTOR THE INSPECTOR
ADOPTED FROM BAD RAP

Because of his great demeanor, Hector, after evaluation, was marked to go to an organization that trains law dogs. However, Hector was found to be too old for the program, and so he was returned to one of BAD RAP's foster homes. Andrew "Roo" & Clara Yori, who adopted him, were the perfect candidates, given the Yoris' work with their pit bull Wallace (*see pgs. 128 & 129*). Despite having physical scars that cover his body from his time at Bad Newz Kennels, Hector shows no psychological or emotional scars. He needed no rehabilitation except for some time adjusting to a home environment, such as learning that plants are not chew toys. A sweet and confident dog who loves to please, adorable Hector now lives the good life. He shares his home with five other dogs, where he lets Mindy Lou, a little 12-lb. toy Australian Shepherd, boss him around all day and naps with his best friend, a Rat Terrier mix named Scooby Snack. He enjoys running around the house with a toy in his mouth, sunning himself and eating vegetables. Hector has no trust issues, loves people and dogs, is a certified therapy dog, has twice earned his Canine Good Citizen certificate and passed the ATTS temperament test. Hector & Wallace both do their part to educate the public about "all dogs labeled as 'pit bulls'" and even have their own website (pitbullunited.com) and Facebook fan pages. Hector visits elementary schools teaching children compassion toward animals and how to act safely around dogs. Hector is quite happy to have Roo hold him in his arms while schoolchildren surround them to scratch Hector's face and rub his belly. Hector's work earned him a humane education award presented through Brooklyn Law School. His story has been highlighted in both local and national media outlets, including, CBS's *The Early Show*, *Good Day New York*, *People*, *E! Entertainment News*, *Parade*, *Entertainment Weekly* and NPR's *Fresh Air*. Hector cares less about the media attention and more about the best gift he was ever given: a chance to be a good dog in a loving home. Hector's scarring speaks volumes about his horrific time at Bad Newz Kennels. However, his remarkable ability to forget his past, trust people and dogs, forgive all that has happened to him and move on to enjoy life provides us with a blueprint for the way we should live our lives. The Yoris said, "Hector is getting a second chance, and he's proving he deserves every moment of it. Hopefully, people will continue to be open to the many lessons Hector can teach us."

140

HALLE

UTAH
LOVES OTHER ANIMALS, PLAYING WITH OTHER DOGS & SWIMMING
ADOPTED FROM BEST FRIENDS ANIMAL SOCIETY (BFAS)

People love Halle; she has such a sweet face and a forgiving spirit. They cannot believe that she spent the first three to four years of her life in such an abusive environment. Halle was used primarily for breeding at Bad Newz Kennels. During the evaluations, she was so dog friendly that she became the dog the staff used to test other dogs. When Traci Madson told friends and family that she was going to adopt one of the Vick dogs, most tried to talk her out of it, stating the dogs would be damaged, unpredictable and not trustworthy. Traci is glad she did not listen to any of them. Halle was the first of the Vicktory dogs at BFAS to be ready for adoption. BFAS thought that Halle and Tacoma (*see pg. 107*), whom Traci had adopted from BFAS six months prior, would be a good match. Tacoma has been a great role model for Halle, who was at first so shy she would tremble when people tried to pet her and would only wag her tail when she saw a dog. When Traci took the dogs places, Halle would "pancake" on the ground, not moving until she saw Tacoma go first. When Tacoma was with her, she was willing to try new things. Halle gains confidence daily. She may always be on the shy side, but now she will sit by people to get petted. If they stop petting her, she will either nudge or paw at them so they will pet her more. She goes to events to help educate people about pit bulls and can do everything for her Canine Good Citizen certificate, as long as she is at home where she feels safe.

142

CHERRY GARCIA

A WORLD-CLASS CUDDLER WITH A HEART OF GOLD, CHERRY ADORES OTHER ANIMALS
ADOPTED FROM BEST FRIENDS ANIMAL SOCIETY (BFAS)

Because of the bad scars on Cherry's back, it is believed he was a bait dog. One of the most traumatized of the Vick dogs, Cherry was sent to BFAS. He would not go on walks when he first arrived; he was shut down. Paul saw him on an episode of *DogTown* on the National Geographic Channel and put in an application. He told his wife, Melissa, the next day and added, "Don't worry! We don't have a shot of being picked." After a year-long application process, they went to Utah with their pit bull mix, Madison, to meet him. They were perfect for each other. Cherry came to them 1.5 weeks later, and his new life began. Madison was exactly the "sister" he needed to help him overcome his past and learn to be a dog. Cherry loves animals and goes to doggy day care. He gains confidence, learns so much from animals and forgets his past when he is with them. Cherry still has extreme psychological issues. He is scared of strangers, especially males, and will "pancake" to the ground when scared. However, he has come far and now has a zest for life. Cherry attends events to educate about pit bulls and dog fighting, has been on television and in books and has his own Facebook page. His story has touched many people and continues to influence others. Paul said, "That has been one of the coolest things...to hear from complete strangers how [Cherry] has taught them about pit bulls and dogs in general...that they adopted a pit bull because of Cherry... We have had family who were unsure when we adopted a pit bull but now are proud...Cherry's story and overall character draw people to him and leave them full of love. He is such a special dog."

HANDSOME DAN

RHODE ISLAND
CHAMPION SNUGGLER & DOTING NANNY DOG
AKA DANSOME, DANIMAL, THE DANIMAL, BUBBA & HANDY
ADOPTED FROM BEST FRIENDS ANIMAL SOCIETY (BFAS)

Dan spent the first 18 months of his life chained outside at Bad Newz Kennels. It is not believed he was fought, since he has no visible scars, which, along with his good looks, got him his name. Dan's scars are all internal. Past emotional and psychological trauma has caused him to be fearful. His health issues include many broken teeth, a cataract in one eye and bowleggedness, which gives him pain in his legs. He is also Babesia positive. Very shy and fearful of people at the time of evaluation, Dan was one of the 22 dogs sent to BFAS. At the sanctuary, his caregiver Betsy Kidder and trainer John Garcia taught him to trust people. Heather Gutshall & Mark Stoutzenberger fostered to adopt Dan through BFAS. Dan has adjusted well to family life with the home's two other dogs and two children, Cam and 15-month-old Josephine. Dan is a doting nanny to the baby. He sleeps next to her crib while she naps and does not budge until she is awake. Dan inspired the family to start Handsome Dan's Rescue for Pit Bull Type Dogs for victims of dog fighting and abuse. He helps to acclimate the home's many foster dogs and helps Heather, a dog trainer, socialize her clients' dogs. Dan finds comfort in routine and familiarity but changes people's opinions of pit bull type dogs every day, especially through his Facebook page, where photos of him being his gentle self with baby Josephine are displayed.

PIPER

VIRGINIA
PLAYFUL PIPER'S FAVORITE WORDS ARE "MUNCHIE," "KITCHEN" & "HUNGRY"
ADOPTED FROM ANIMAL RESCUE OF TIDEWATER (ART)

Piper (formerly known as "Sox") was one of the worst of the low-response dogs at the time of evaluation. She could hardly open her eyes and was unable to focus. The team discussed euthanasia as an option. However, Piper has Babesia, and it is now thought that she might have been experiencing a bad spike in symptoms that day. Piper was fostered and trained by Rhoda & Charles Tucker, who also run a doggy day care. When Piper first came to them, she reminded them of a skateboard with legs scurrying around remaining low to the ground and with no real direction; she was too terrified to stop moving. Three months into her rehabilitation she was practically cured of that. However, one day, one of the day-care dogs got his foot caught and wailed in pain. The dog's screaming terrified Piper, who sat on a step, her entire body vibrating, too scared to move. Rhoda said, "I don't think I will ever be able to remember it without tears, no matter how far we have come." And they have come very far. Whenever a situation scares Piper, Rhoda uses trigger phrases to let Piper know to relax and that everything is OK. Piper has earned her Canine Good Citizen certificate and is certified as a therapy dog. She also works as a reading-assistance dog for children. Piper is part of the Drill Team for the Pit Bull Awareness Coalition, performing commands to music, marching in parades and spreading awareness in places where pit bull type dogs are feared or abused. Piper was adopted by Nancy Hensley-Hill. She now lives happily with her canine "brothers" and "sisters," a parrot and a cat. She goes to day care where she plays with dogs of all breeds and sizes. Piper is a comical, loving, sweet dog who loves children and is eager to please, especially for treats. She is happy and loved.

GRACIE

VIRGINIA
LOVES TO BE WITH OTHER DOGS & ADORES HER "BROTHER" PETEY, A KATRINA PIT BULL
AKA CHUNKY MONKEY & GOO GOO DOG
ADOPTED FROM RICHMOND ANIMAL LEAGUE (RAL)

It is believed Gracie was used as a breeding dog at Bad Newz Kennels. One of the few dogs sent to RAL, she was 3 years old when Sharon Cornett adopted her. At Sharon's house, Gracie is living the good life with six other dogs and a few cats. Here, Gracie has found her niche in life: to help other abused dogs overcome the adversities they have endured. Last year, Sharon took in a foster beagle who was seized in a cruelty case. The dog was terrified of everything and everyone. From the first night the beagle was there, Gracie sensed that all was not right, and appointed herself the dog's guardian angel. They sleep on the sofa together, and Gracie always lies in front, almost as if she is letting the beagle know that she will protect her. She has helped the beagle come out of her shell and feel more confident. Gracie is also doing her part to change people's opinions of pit bulls and dogs from fight busts. She has made many public appearances and now has a pit bull rescue group named after her. Gracie's Guardians, a division of RAL, has a mission to show the public that they have nothing to fear from pit bulls. When not making a public appearance, this couch potato spends her days sleeping on the sofa—her favorite pastime. It is her job is to "guard the remote" to make sure the cats do not tamper with it. She loves other dogs. Cats? She tolerates them.

JHUMPA JONES

NEW YORK
JHUMPA LOVES STRING CHEESE, RIDING IN THE CAR, SNUGGLING & GIVING KISSES
AKA THE LITTLE ENGINE THAT COULD
ADOPTED FROM RICHMOND ANIMAL LEAGUE (RAL) & OUT OF THE PITS (OOTP)

Originally placed with RAL, Jhumpa Jones was shipped to New York to a rescue that had a foster home in place. However, when that home fell through, Jhumpa then sat kenneled at a veterinary office with little interaction. Her condition soon deteriorated. Kathleen Pierce heard about her and stepped in to adopt her. Jhumpa had been at Bad Newz Kennels, then held as evidence for months and then kenneled at the vet's. Needless to say, her condition was not great. She was overwhelmingly shy and even the daily routine was a challenge. However, she showed Kathleen that her past would not define her—she slowly overcame her fears. She now lives with her family of four canine "siblings," including big "brother" Pig (see pg. 125), and several cats. She loves to lounge in the grass, roasting her bones in the sun, and she spins with excitement when Kathleen comes in the door. Jhumpa has begun playing the role of foster "sister" to other rescued dogs that are now beginning their new lives. Jhumpa sleeps with sound contentment, often snoring. She is probably best known for her expressive ears that go on and on; they will "tent" together to make a pointed peak at the top of her head when she is showing interest in something, like a set of antennae picking up a signal. Jhumpa has earned her Canine Good Citizen certificate and is a certified therapy dog.

152

Myth #1: Pit bulls are mean and vicious. Pit bulls pass the ATTS's temperament test at a rate similar to, if not higher than, many other similar-sized, strong breeds. The APBT, AST and SBT* pass at rates of 84.3 percent, 83.4 percent, and 88.8 percent, respectively. Compare this to Golden Retrievers (84.2 percent), Great Danes (79.2 percent) and Weimaraners (80.1 percent). Carl Herkstroeter, the president of the ATTS, has commented on these results: "We have tested somewhere around 1,000 pit bull type dogs....I've tested half of them. And of the number I've tested I have disqualified one pit bull because of aggressive tendencies. They have done extremely well. They have a good temperament. They are very good with children."

Myth #2: Pit bulls have locking jaws. No mammals, including pit bulls, have locking jaws.

Myth #3: Pit bulls have massive biting power. There is no scientific evidence that any kind of dog bites differently than any other. While bite force cannot be reliably determined in dogs, professionals concur that dogs bite with a force of 200 psi to 450 psi, depending on the dog's size. *(National Canine Research Council)*

Myth #4: Pit bulls will become aggressive & turn on their owners. They are predisposed to be aggressive to humans. Human aggression is not a trait attributed to ASTs, SBTs or APBTs. It is never considered to be acceptable behavior in those breeds.

Myth #5: Pit bulls are dog aggressive by nature. We are doing pit bull type dogs a disservice assuming they will be dog aggressive. Each dog should be evaluated individually.

Myth #6: A pit bull that shows aggression toward animals will go after people next. Canine aggression toward dogs and canine aggression toward humans are entirely unrelated. They do not cross over.

Myth #7: Pit bulls do not feel pain. Dog fighters have promoted this idea to excuse their abuse of these dogs. Every dog feels pain.

Myth #8: Pit bulls with scars or cropped ears were used for dog fighting. Dogs get scars from all kinds of injuries, not just dog fighting. Rather than speculate about how a dog got scarred, evaluate the dog to see whether his/her past has affected the dog's demeanor. Scars do not predict behavior.

Myth #9: Pit bulls are not good with kids. Well-socialized dogs of all kinds do well around children. Supervision between dogs and children is always a must in any setting. It is also important to teach children how to interact with animals properly.

American Pit Bull Terrier (APBT), American Staffordshire Terrier (AST), Staffordshire Bull Terrier (SBT)

RESCUES, ADVOCACY GROUPS & EDUCATIONAL WEBSITES

Animal Farm Foundation | animalfarmfoundation.org
BAD RAP | badrap.org
Best Friends Animal Society | bestfriends.org
Cuda Cares | facebook.com/cudacaresorg
Dogs Deserve Better | dogsdeservebetter.org
Elderbulls | elderbulls.blogspot.com
Our Pack | ourpack.org
Pinups for Pitbulls | pinupsforpitbulls.com
Pit Bull Rescue Central | pbrc.net
Pit Bull United | pitbullunited.com

Utley Foundation | theutleyfoundation.com
StubbyDog | stubbydog.org
Sula Foundation | sulafoundation.org
Villalobos Rescue Center | vrcpitbull.com

Websites on the Vick Dogs
BAD RAP | badrap.org/rescue/vick
Best Friends Animal Society | bestfriends.org/vickdogs
Pit Bull United | hectorthepitbull.com
Vick Dog Blog | vickdogsblog.blogspot.com

BOOKS
One Hour With Patrick by Jeff Coltenback
Oogy: The Dog Only a Family Could Love by Larry Levin
The Pit Bull Placebo by Karen Delise
Shelby's Grace: From Abused Pup to Angel of Mercy by Joe Dwyer

Books on the Vick Dogs
The Lost Dogs by Jim Gorant
Saving Audie: A Pit Bull Puppy Gets a Second Chance by Dorothy Hinshaw Patent & William Muñoz

FILMS
Wallace the Pit Bull: The Rise of an Underdog

THE PROJECTS WISH TO THANK THE FOLLOWING BUSINESSES & ORGANIZATIONS FOR THEIR SUPPORT

ANIMAL HOSPITAL

Quarry Hill Park Animal Hospital — Rochester, MN

ANIMAL RESCUE, EDUCATION & ADVOCACY

Angel City Pit Bulls — Los Angeles, CA angelcitypits.org (a non-profit, breed specific rescue organization)
Animal Rescue Front, USA — animalrescuefront.org (animal rescue & transport non-profit)
BAMBA (Bully Advocates of the Monterey Bay Area)
Best Friends Animal Society — Kanab, UT bestfriends.org (leading the way toward no more homeless pets®)
Bully Breed Rescue Inc. — New Canaan, CT bullybreedrescueinc.org (pit bull rescue)
Daisy Davis Pit Bull Rescue — Fort Bragg, CA Thank you Daisy Davis for changing my world & inspiring the start of a rescue, to help other pit bulls in need! I love you Daisy!!! (animal rescue)
I'm Not a Monster — imnotamonster.org (good dog advocacy organization)
Love is The Pits — Oceanside, CA loveisthepits.com (bullied breeds advocates)
Mohawk Hudson Humane Society — Albany, NY mohawkhumane.org
Pit Stop Montreal Rescue — Montreal, Canada pitstopmontreal.com (pit bull rescue)
Power Breed Rescue — Palouse, WA For Jamie & Dice who started it all
Prairie Pit Bull Rescue Society — Alberta, Canada prairiepitbullrescue.com
Presidential Pits — Washington, DC area presidentialpits.org (pit bull type dog rescue & advocacy)
Ruff Road Rescue — Mesa, AZ ruffroadrescue.com (dog rescue)
San Benito Bullies — Hollister, CA sanbenitobullies.wordpress.com (pit bull education & advocacy group)
Sarge the Elderbull — elderbulls.blogspot.com
Save-a-Bull — mohawkhumanesociety.org (pit bull awareness program of MHHS)
Starfish to the Sea Animal Rescue — Southwestern PA (animal rescue)

ARTISTS & PHOTOGRAPHERS

Hany Hosny Photography — Roanoke, VA hanyhosnyphotography.com (sports & travel photography)
Stephen James Photography — Philadelphia, PA facebook.com/StephenJamesPhotography (photographer)
Martha Kennedy Studio — Santa Fe, NM marthakennedy.com (artist)
Pet Portraits by Ann Ranlett — petportraitsbyann.com (pet portraits & gifts)

CLOTHING

Cotton Factory — Pittsburgh, PA cottonfactory.com (hand silk-screened apparel)

CONSULTING SERVICES

ShelTek, Inc. — Minneapolis, MN sheltek.us (IT consulting services)
True Voices, Inc. — truevoices.com (certified coaching, consulting, courage)

DOG BOOK/ AUTHOR

Joe Dwyer, *Shelby's Grace: From Abused Pup to Angel of Mercy* — shelbysgrace.com (author & speaker)

DOG MEET-UP GROUPS

The Monmouth County Underdogs — Monmouth County, NJ facebook.com/monmouthcountyunderdogs & meetup.com/monmouth-county-under-dogs (NJ-based social & educational meetup group)
NYC Pit Bull Group (Amy Calmann) — meetup.com/NYC-Pitbull

DOG TRAINING

AngelDogs Training — Santa Clarita, CA angeldogstraining.com (CPDT dog training, CGC evaluator)

EXERCISE & PROTEIN

Danza Mystique — The Magic of Dance, Des Moines, IA danzamystique.com (bellydancing group)
SMS High Performance Weight Gainer — Los Angeles, CA sizemassstrength.com & our little rescue Rambo! (protein)

PET ACCESSORIES

Aunt Betty's Aprons — San Jose, CA auntbettysaprons@gmail.com (custom items for you & your pet)
Collar Me Up — Rochester, NY collarmeup.com (handmade custom dog collars)
girl.bike.dog. — Philadelphia, PA girlbikedog.com (handmade messenger bags & dog accessories)

PET FOOD & PRODUCTS

The Big Bad Woof — Washington, DC thebigbadwoof.com (holistic, eco-friendly pet supply store)
Crunchies Natural Pet Foods — Crofton, MD crunchies.com (natural pet food retailer)
Nature's Select Pet Food of Ft. Worth — Ft Worth/Tarrant County, TX txpetfood.com (home delivery of holistic & all-natural pet food & products)

PET SITTING

Amanda's Pet Care — Arlington, VA amandaspetcare.com
Paw Buddiez — Los Angeles, CA pawbuddiez.com (professional experienced pet care)
Peace of Mind Pet Sitters — Sandy, UT peaceofmindpetsitters.biz (pet sitter & dog walker)
PetsitUSA.com — petsitusa.com (pet sitters)

OTHER

The American Bully Kennel Club (ABKC) — theabkcdogs.com
Beacon Title Services Agency, Inc. — Serving Southern New Jersey
The Camber Group — New Berlin, WI thecambergroup.net (proud sponsors of CudaCares.org, a little pit bull with a big heart sharing an important message)
Mick Manley II Insurance — Omaha, NE
Students of Cunningham Creek Elementary School — Fruit Cove, FL
Suburbia Roller Derby — Yonkers, NY suburbiarollerderby.com
Three Monkeys Cafe (Mike & Jackie McDonald) — East Torresdale, Philadelphia, PA
Top 40 Music, LLC — Mahopac, NY top40musicgroup.com
For our loving pit bulls DaVinci, Max & all the pits in need, we love you

THE PROJECTS WISH TO THANK THE FOLLOWING PEOPLE FOR THEIR SUPPORT

For our pit bull Abigail
Julee & Brett Allen, In loving memory of Zuzu — Seattle, WA
Susi Allen, For Bunny, the little pit bull that changed my life forever — Monterey, CA
Sherri Alston, For my first pittie love Tank
Andrew, Cori, Quilla & Saracen — Chicago, IL
The Andrews Family, For our pit bulls Sarah & Sally — Chattanooga, TN
Tina Austin & "The Hairbabies," Missy, Bandit, Reily & Callie — Tacoma, WA
The Ayers Family, In loving memory of Hogan
Adam & Carrie Aylor, For all our pit bull fosters — Arvada, CO
Mary Balboni
The Barron Family, In loving memory of Teka & Kayzer — Crown Point, IN
Kelley Beaudry — East Providence, RI
In loving memory of my baby pit Brandy (1997-2011)
Natascha Brauss, In memory of all pibbles — Spokane, WA
Robbyn Braverman, For ALL of the pit bulls in my life, especially Hawkeye, "My Son." I will always love you the very most.
Carol Brown & Kevin Elmore — Lubbock, TX
Rick, Mary Beth & Ozzy Brown — St. Louis, MO
Tony Brown & Kembree Darakshani Brown, In celebration of our pit bull dogs, Lennox & Lane — Memphis, TN
Denise Buckheister & Michael Smith — Grapevine, TX
Anne Burke, In memory of all my wonderful pit bulls who have crossed the Rainbow Bridge — Cleveland, OH
Jody Burnett
Shalia, Manny & Willow Buxton — Truckee, CA
Amanda, Steven & Zuma Carlson — Arlington, VA
Cass & Linc, For Bud & Jax — Rehoboth Beach, DE
Clare Cassar, In memory of Sarge — Cheltenham, UK
In memory of Paul J. Channell, Jr., whose time loving animals was cut short — Santa Fe, NM
Charlotte, thank you for introducing me to pit bulls & educating me. I love you always!
Susan Chesson, In honor of my bullies, Gemma & Ruby, & all of the animals who have inspired me to do more — Greenville, NC
Jeff & Stacey, Winnie & Jack Clark — Montclair, NJ
The Clayton Family Pack, For our sweet pit bull Sunny — Houston, TX area
Andrew Michael Cook, For Chloe & the unconditional love she provides — Macon, GA
Bobby & Elaine Cowley, For Dov — Midland, TX
Lisa Culver, In memory of sweet Gretchen
Thank you, Cutter, for letting us be your humans. We love you — Burt & Tom
The Cyrs, In memory of Choco Taco — Jacksonville, FL
Connie DeFrance, I love my pit bulls Bailey & Karma — Herndon, VA
Devon & Nathan, For our pit bull Bowser
The Di Ilio Family, In memory of all BSL victims! — Ottawa, ON, Canada
In memory of Doogie
The Drabek Family — Lewisville, TX
Duhamel & Tetrault Family, For our "kids" Roxy & Churchill — Watertown & New Haven, CT
Anna Dunn, In memory of Bird — Brooklyn, NY
Rachel Erickson CVT, With love from my ratties, Jonas & Theo — Rochester, MN
The Fairchild Family, For our pit bulls Georgia & RoRo — Seattle, WA
The Federowicz Family, For our bullies, Farts & Beasley — Boothwyn, PA
Georgette Fernandez
The five extraordinary dogs who inspire Kathleen Pierce — Albany, NY
Genie & Dave Folsom, In honor of all the dogs we have saved who in turn saved us
Ida Fong, For all the pit bulls out there
Mike Funnell — Sydney, Australia
Frank & Nicole Gallo, In memory of Tiny, the greatest dog who ever lived. We miss you buddy roo — Rahway, NJ
Bobby Gambino & Roxie — San Mateo, CA
Tankgirl Ginsburg-Streibig — Pittsburgh, PA
The Green Family, For our beloved pit bulls, Shania, Uno & Memphis — Cherokee, AL
Stacey Greenwald, For my pit bull & best friend Wilson — Atlanta, GA
Falon Greer & my snuggle buddy, Mattie — Chicago, IL
Matthew & Kirsten Greskiewicz, For our bullies Minka & Batman
Eric & Kathy Gross, for our best friend Petey — Enfield, CT
Kristi Gross, Gypsy & Panda — Dallas, TX
Jennifer Hart, For Hilda
Doug & Jenny Hartwig, For the pittie who stole our hearts, Lyla — Carlsbad, CA
Cynthia Hayes, oneyedog
To Haylie, Henry & Goody my best pibble fur friends, Love Julian — Vernon, NJ
The Hendrix Family — Roswell, NM
Susan Herring + K9 kids, Kita & Saydee — Montgomery, IL
Jim, Alice, Ryan, Tillie & Shady Jackson — Spicewood, TX
In memory of Jake
Jim & Suzanne, For our other pittie, Rufus — Sacramento, CA
Francesca Kennedy, In memory of Googie, Bow & Dory
Susan Kessler, Advocate for equal treatment & opportunity for "pit bull" dogs
Kari Kilgore, For Bella, who rescued me — St. Paul, VA
Sydney Killian, For my wonderful Wesley
The Kim Family, We love you, Charlie! — New York, NY

Michael & Candice Kirsten, For our adorable Boston/Pit mix Addy — New York, NY
Penny & Rich Kluko, In memory of Sweetie & Cutie — Bay Shore, NY
Kohler/Moldovan Family, For Sam, Dave & Stella who bring us joy every day
Joe Kotch, In honor of Bella, Nina, Sula & Shadow, & in memory of Sage
The Larssons — Seattle, WA
Lisa & Menotti, For our pit bull Primo — New York, NY
Ivy Loh & my elderjacks, Jesus & Momo — Singapore
Kerri Lopes & Mark Ready, For Marco — Dighton, MA
The Lueckfeld Family, Because we love pit bulls — Sunnyvale, CA
Ellen McCloskey — Chesterfield, MO
Jena McFall, In loving memory of Jack the Ripper
Traci Madson & Tacoma, Halle & Jasmine
The Malveiro Family, For our amazing dog Lucy — Warminster, PA
Alvin N. Mangosing, For my lovely Lucy — Seattle, WA
Marc & Mayr, Taco & Betty — Greenfield, MA
The Masseys, For our sweet pit Raven — Strasburg, CO
Elizabeth & Michael Massaro, In honor of the 2 brightest little lights in our lives, Arnold & Cammie. Little C & BG, we love you both so much! — Marlton, NJ
Irma Mendoza & Eloy Hernandez, In honor of Boonies, our love of our lives — Austin, TX
Merlin shepherd-lab-chow-bull, precious fur-kid — July 23, 1997 — Forever my heart
For Mr. Brown, the little bully we rescued & who buried himself deep into our hearts
For Molly, Henry, Roscoe & Jojo
Carla Moreno, For Bruce & Nacho — Orange County, CA
Kelly Morton, On behalf of Anita Stombock & in memory of Blaze — Jacksonville, FL
Laura & Gary Mudrow, Vishnu & Zoey, In memory of Tyler, Shai & Cody — Atlanta, GA
Bryan & April Myers, For our friendly little pits, Hope & Dozer — Baltimore, MD
Laura Myers, In memory of Bailey — Rowlett, TX
Jussi Myllyluoma — Sweden
For our "pibble" Nakia, hugs & kisses forever! Love James & J-Bug
Nicole Nichols, Ryan Jensen & The 12 Feet, In honor of our boy Kirby — Gainesville, FL
Amanda Nieves, For Lily — Clearwater Beach, FL
In honor of the Norfolk SPCA, VB SPCA & Forever-Home Sanctuary, The Smith Pack (Jack, pit bull Roxie, Misty & Jennifer) loves you!
Jenn Nourse, In memory of Lucy, Pepper, Sam & Newman — Seattle, WA
Jack & Dee O'Brien, To honor our current pit Arizona & all those that have passed before him — Gloversville, NY
Joe & Brandy Ochoa & our pit bulls Piper, Jackson & Jersey — Lone Jack, MO
Karen Pederson, For ALL pit bulls — Riverside, CA
The Pelliccios, In honor of Leroix & Nola — Branford CT
Barbara Perez — Hudson, FL
Bill & Daryl Pierce, In honor of Jhumpa Jones & Pig
In memory of Phillip Fair, beloved pittie — Wenonah, NJ
Anita Pinner, In loving memory of Heavy Chevy & Mr. Leo
Erin & Maddie Ramsey
Gerhard Reimann-Basch
Dianne Louise Rhodes — Washington, DC
Lisa Riefer & Lisa Ferlita, In memory of Dexter — New Berlin, WI
BJ & Cookie Q Rodriguez, In loving memory of Sarge Wolf-Stringer — Philadelphia, PA
The Rombeau Family, For Franklin & in memory of Rocky — Philadelphia, PA
The Rosenberg Family — Bainbridge Island, WA
Tom & Aimee Ross, In memory of Merlin & Razzie — Abingdon, MD
Vanity Rossman aka Miss Wigglebottoms — Cleveland, OH
The Rouzeau Family, In memory of Deena's Crystal girl — Jacksonville, FL
The Sauer Family, For our awesome pit bull Angus
The Scardera Family, For our pit bull Murphy — Mahopac, NY
Mike & Shelley Seitz, In honor of Piglet — Little Rock, AR
Mike & Shelley Seitz, In memory of Luna Belle — Little Rock, AR
Scott & Veronica Selco & the Bully Brigade — Las Vegas, NV
Kelley Simon & Todd Bingnear — Gilbertsville, PA
Charlotte Skey — Orange County, CA
The Solomon Family, For our pit bull Herbie — Newport Beach, CA
Mark & Angie Sorensen — Atlanta, GA
Stout-Delabres — Lower Gwynedd, PA
Suzanne & Jim, For our sweet pittie Mickey — Sacramento, CA
Michael & Sue Sweeney — Prior Lake, MN
Curtis & Cyndi Tadehara — Salt Lake City, UT
The Tadlock Family with Echo the Deaf Pittie, For pit bulls everywhere — Fort Bragg, CA
Kat & Kris Tatur — South Tamworth, NH
Linda Thornton, For Alex (her person) — Brooklyn, NY
Tricia & DJ, Bobbi, Suzi, & Alex, For our pit bull Dodger — Oklahoma City, OK
Michelle Tuinstra, For my pit bulls Montana & Jasmine
Janice & Willy & Savannah & Rayna & Paco Tuzcan, In memory of Sailor & Skipper
Uba, For all the dogs still suffering the cruelty of dog fighting
The Visic Family, In cherished memory of Phoebe the Roo — Phoenix, AZ
Jenny Walker, For Kain — East Palo Alto, CA
The Wallace Pups, Casey, Lily, Fred & Pittie Fiona — Philadelphia, PA
Alex & Ben Walldeczka, For Lollie Wonderdog & all our foster bullies — Takoma Park, MD
Manda & Alan Whitehurst, For Petey, our pit bull angel in Heaven. We'll always love you. You'll live forever in our hearts! Puppy kisses & cheeseburger wishes, Kya & Louey
Juliana Willems, For my first foster bully Otis — Rockville, MD

THE FOLLOWING ENTITIES ARE RESPONSIBLE FOR SAVING THE DOGS IN THIS BOOK

animal care & control of NYC, manhattan | nycacc.org
animal farm foundation | animalfarmfoundation.org
animal friends | thinkingoutsidethecage.org
animal haven | animalhavenshelter.org
animal orphanage | theanimalorphanage.org
animal rescue league of western pa | animalrescue.org
animal rescue of tidewater | artanimals.org
ardmore animal hospital | ardmoreah.com
austin humane society | austinhumanesociety.org
austin pets alive | austinpetsalive.org
bad rap | badrap.org
best friends animal society | bestfriends.org
bloomfield animal shelter
chako pit bull rescue | chako.org
colorado pit bull rescue | coloradopitbullrescue.com
companion pet rescue & transport | cprdogs.com
euless animal control | eulesstx.gov/animal
gentle souls sanctuary | gentlesoulssanctuary.org
handsome dan's rescue | obhounds.com/HandsomeDansRescue.aspx
humane society of the pikes peak region | hsppr.org
karma rescue | karmarescue.org
mendocino coast humane society | mendocinohumane.org
monmouth county spca | monmouthcountyspca.org
montgomery county humane society | mchumane.org
northcentral working dog club | northcentralworkingdogclub.com
open arms resq & refurral | petfinder.com/shelters/PA460.html
out of the pits | outofthepits.org
oxford animal shelter | petfinder.com/~CT57
peanut's place bully rescue | peanutsplacebullyrescue.org
pennsylvania spca | pspca.org
pet rescue of mercer | petrescueofmercer.org
pitty rescue | pittyrescue.org
recycled canines dalmatian rescue | recycledcanines.org
richmond animal league | ral.org
santa cruz county animal services | scanimalservices.us
seattle animal shelter | seattleanimalshelter.org
secondhand snoots rescue | secondhandsnoots.org
smiley dog rescue | smileydogrescue.org
smilin' pit bull rescue | spbr.org
staffordshire bull terrier club of america (staffordshire bull terrier rescue) | sbtca.com
street tails animal rescue | streettails.org
town lake animal center | petfinder.com/shelters/TX514.html
watermelon mountain ranch | wmranch.org